Today I Gave Myself Permission to Dream

Race and Incarceration in America

Edited by Erin Brigham
and Kimberly Rae Connor

Published by the
UNIVERSITY OF SAN FRANCISCO PRESS
Joan and Ralph Lane Center
for Catholic Studies and Social Thought

University of San Francisco
2130 Fulton Street
San Francisco, CA 94117-1080
www.usfca.edu/lane-center

Collection copyright © 2018 | ISBN 978-1-947826-71-7

Authors retain the copyright to their individual essays. Queries regarding permissions should be sent to the authors using the email addresses provided with their essays.

Published by the University of San Francisco Press through the Joan and Ralph Lane Center for Catholic Studies and Social ought of the University of San Francisco.

The Lane Center Series promotes the center's mission to advance the scholarship and application of the Catholic intellectual tradition in the church and society with an emphasis on social concerns. The series features essays by Lane Center scholars, guest speakers, and USF faculty. It serves as a written archive of Lane Center events and programs and allows the work of the center to reach a broader audience.

Cover: *Waning Hope,* Juan Carlos Tercero, acrylic, 12x20 inches, Lancaster State Prison [year of creation unknown].

The Lane Center Series

Published by the Joan and Ralph Lane Center for Catholic Studies and Social Thought at the University of San Francisco, the Lane Center Series explores intersections of faith and social justice. Featuring essays that bridge interdisciplinary research and community engagement, the series serves as a resource for social analysis, theological reflection, and education in the Jesuit tradition.

Visit the Lane Center's website to download each volume and view related resources at www.usfca.edu/lane-center

Volumes

Islam at Jesuit Colleges and Universities

Pope Francis and the Future of Catholicism in the United States: The Challenge of Becoming a Church for the Poor

The Declaration on Christian Education: Reflections by the Institute for Catholic Educational Leadership and the Joan and Ralph Lane Center for Catholic Studies and Social Thought

Dorothy Day: A Life and Legacy

Editor

Erin Brigham
Lane Center, University of San Francisco

Editorial Board

KIMBERLY RAE CONNOR
School of Management, University of San Francisco

THERESA LADRIGAN-WHELPLEY
Ignatian Center for Jesuit Education, Santa Clara University

CATHERINE PUNSALAN MANLIMOS
Institute for Catholic Thought and Culture, Seattle University

LISA FULLAM
Jesuit School of Theology of Santa Clara University

DONAL GODFREY, S.J.
University Ministry, University of San Francisco

MARK MILLER
Department of Theology and Religious Studies,
University of San Francisco

MARK POTTER
Newton Country Day School of the Sacred Heart, Newton MA

FRANK TURNER, S.J.
Delegate for the Jesuit Intellectual Apostolate, London

Table of Contents

Acknowledgements...7

Forward..9
WILLIAM O'NEILL, S.J. AND ERIN BRIGHAM

Dream..15
REGGIE DANIELS

Why are Racial Minorities Overrepresented
in the Prison Population?
A Systemic Institutional Inquiry...19
HADAR AVIRAM

Where You Can't Be Colorblind:
Race, Incarceration, and Reentry 33
KIMBERLY RICHMAN

Reconstructing the Moral Claim
of Racially Unjust Mass Incarceration......................................47
ALISON BENDERS

Envisioning Social Justice:
From Theory to Practice 59
REGGIE DANIELS

Art Between the Bars:
In Search of Self and Fellowship 69
LARRY BREWSTER AND CUONG TRAN

Our Racist Reality: How Ignatian Spirituality Can
Help Inmates and Prison Ministers Positively Deal with the
Stressors of Racism in an Inmate's Life 83
JOHN BOOTH

Truth Is 97
ALISHA COLEMAN

Afterward 101
MARY WARDELL

Acknowledgements

We would like to thank each participant in the Lane Center's 2017 Roundtable on Race and Incarceration and the following community partners who made it possible: California Coalition of Women Prisoners, Thrive for Life Prison Ministry, the Jesuit Conference of Canada and the United States, and Homeboy Industries. Thank you to the artists who contributed to this volume and to Peter Merts for his photography of their artwork. We are grateful for the ongoing work of the Arts-in-Corrections program. Thank you to Larry Brewster and William O'Neill, S.J. for helping us imagine the shape of the volume and stay true to the vision of the roundtable. And finally, thank you to Alyssa Perez for organizing, copyediting, and moving the volume toward publication.

Forward

WILLIAM O'NEILL, SJ
AND ERIN BRIGHAM

The fate of millions of people—indeed the future of the black community itself—may depend on the willingness of those who care about racial justice to re-examine their basic assumptions about the role of the criminal justice system in our society.[1]

By exposing how the criminal justice system functions to systematically oppress people of color in the United States, Michelle Alexander has highlighted the urgency of our need for a structural and cultural transformation. Writers such as Alexander, as well as activists in the Black Lives Matter movement, have demonstrated that it is not enough to care about racial justice; one needs to undergo a process of unlearning false assumptions about power and punishment in the United States. Moving from a retributive view of justice toward one that seeks to restore right relationships among the entire community necessitates that we undertake an honest re-examination of race and the criminal justice system in our society.

Jesuit institutions are positioned to promote this transformation through their commitment to social justice in teaching and research that leads by listening to the voices of marginalized people working to dismantle systems of oppression. We do so mindful of what Reggie

---

[1] Michelle Alexander, *The New Jim Crow: Mass Incarceration in the Age of Colorblindness* (New York: The New Press, 2010, 2012), 16.

Daniels, a formerly incarcerated scholar and artist, has pointed out in this volume: the knowledge that is generated outside of the university can also expose limitations and blind-spots within academic institutions.

The Lane Center's *2017 Roundtable on Race and Incarceration* brought together the wisdom of formerly incarcerated activists and leaders with artists, ministers and scholars of various disciplines—law, sociology, theology, critical race theory, and pastoral ministry. Participants investigated the historical, legal, and political structures behind the mass incarceration of people of color in the United States and explored the impact of the criminal justice system on individuals and families while identifying the ethical and theological dimensions of this reality. The intent of the roundtable was to use our Jesuit tradition of consciousness-raising to bridge the resources of the university with those of the community. This book is an expression and expansion of that conversation.

The roundtable and the book give expression to the mission of the *Joan and Ralph Lane Center for Catholic Studies and Social Thought at the University of San Francisco*. Charged with the task of analyzing contemporary social issues, the Center engages critically with religious and secular frameworks of justice—identifying resources as well as areas for development. Situated at a Jesuit university, the Center is accountable to a particular framework of justice that flows from the Catholic social tradition. Within this tradition, social conditions are always evaluated from the reality of the most vulnerable; and the wisdom of those who are marginalized by society is recognized as central to the work of social transformation.

Appropriately, the roundtable created a space for all participants to begin a dialogue on racial justice, reconciliation, and transformation. The discussion not only exposed the historical, social, legal, and ethical dimensions of racial injustice in our prisons; it highlighted the resilience and strategies of resistance among incarcerated and formerly incarcerated individuals. In particular, the conversation and resulting essays lift up the role of spirituality and creative expression as essential to the survival and transformation of incarcerated and formerly incarcerated people.

Inspired by the roundtable and the conversation it engendered, this volume does not seek to offer a comprehensive analysis of the intersections of race and incarceration. Rather, it offers an invitation to participate in the re-examination of the criminal justice system for those of us who care about racial justice and the common good. The first two essays contextualize the reality of racial injustice and mass incarceration in the 21st century. First, Hadar Aviram exposes the disproportionate representation of people of color in U.S. prisons and locates this reality within the history of racial segregation. Writing as a legal scholar, she demonstrates how the institutionalization of racism is evidenced in policing, courtroom procedures, and sentencing. Kimberly Richman picks up where Aviram's analysis leaves off, focusing on the role of race in prisoners' experiences of reentry programs. As a sociologist, Richman outlines the political, social, and economic barriers to reentry that are exacerbated by racism. Reflecting on this context from the perspective of theological ethics, Alison Benders begins with the assertion in Catholic theology that racism is a social sin. She goes on to challenge the reader to consider one's own positionality within a framework of radical interdependence.

The final essays reveal strategies of survival and transformation in the midst of these unjust systems. Reggie Daniels offers a critical evaluation of prison programs that fail to empower participants to access their own wisdom and resources for development. Drawing upon his own experience of incarceration as well as critical race theory and critical pedagogy, Daniels argues for prison programs that subvert the power structure embedded in the prison system. In the next essay, Larry Brewster and Cuong Tran reveal the power of art to subvert the oppressive power structure and build community across barriers that exist among prisoners. Likewise, John Booth discusses the role of Ignatian spirituality in cultivating resilience and resistance to dehumanizing structures in prison. Finally, Mary Wardell returns to the context of Jesuit higher education. Writing as the Chief Diversity Officer for USF, and informed by our Jesuit mission, she offers concrete actions that people working in Jesuit institutions can take to promote solidarity with incarcerated people and counter racism in our institutions and in society. Throughout this volume we have included, between the discursive essays, poems and reproductions of artwork created by individuals while they were incarcerated. We offer these creative expressions of self-definition to illustrate more fully the transformative power this volume hopes to spread.

Anatomy of Birds/Self-Portrait, Omid Mokri, 24 inches diameter; acrylic on tee-shirt, San Quentin State Prison, 2015

Dream

Reggie Daniels[1]

I dream.
My eyes are closed.
But it's not that kind of dream where I am relaxed and sleeping.
I am awake and focused.
Focused on my seeds of hope.
I am watering them,
and I am dreaming and I am nurturing my ideas.

I think big:
International trade industry,
work-business for youth. I have reached for the pie,
and my community has shifted.
My son's future is big with hope.
I was his superman
and he has become my black superhero.

---

[1] Reggie P. Daniels is a Youth Director at the San Francisco Sheriff's Department. He works with incarcerated youth, ages 18-25. KQED recognized his work by awarding him the "Black Hero's Award." He also was recognized by the Bay View Hunters Point Foundation and received the "Change Agent Award" for his personal and professional achievements. His research focuses on in-custody violence prevention program efficacy and culturally responsive pedagogy and policies. His passion is working to interrupt oppressive systems and to bring social justice to his community. Reggie is currently a doctoral candidate at the University of San Francisco.

I concentrate harder because the demons
come to frame my thoughts and ideas,
because I am practically a middle-aged black man,
ex-offender,
ex-drug dealer,
dickslanger,
mind entangler.

And while I was lying on my back
looking up at the sky
surrounded by a bunch of able-bodied men
trapped in a nightmare of
ain'ts can'ts do's and don'ts,
mindless labor that does not land me on the
runway of my dreams…
I fell deep into a trance
when the man with the keys to my freedom told me to dream
and have it ready for him today.

So here is my dream…
The world is a safe place for me and my seeds.
We are no longer treated like the invisible man.
There is a team of experts waiting for my next dream
so they can start putting my thoughts
immediately into action.
Me and my seed walk in the garden and share our dreams
and we don't have to worry about
becoming the next black president
because we have finally figured out that
we are all world leaders.

Happiness is more that just
a hit, a toke, a fix, or a snort.
It's my station in life and now
my goals have a train, a railway

And I am no longer just lying on my back.
Incarcerated, shackled in my mind.
I am free to move forward.
To take flight.
And never look down.

The only way that I will ever know
How high I am is when I hear people say:
Look at him go.
Boy that cat can go.
Look up in the sky,
It's a bird, it's a plane
No—it's another Black Super Man!

My son and I no longer walk when we dream,
We take flight!
Jordan! Today is Father's Day.
And I gave myself a wonderful gift today.
Today I gave myself permission to dream
without excuses.

Why are Racial Minorities Overrepresented in the Prison Population? A Systemic Institutional Inquiry

HADAR AVIRAM[1]

To modern, racially conscious readers and viewers, Margaret Mitchell's novel *Gone with the Wind*,[2] and David O. Selznick's film based on it appear to be indefensible propaganda for the abhorrent ideology of the antebellum South.[3] The many critics of the film tend to ignore one forgotten but important scene. Shortly after the end of the civil war, as Scarlett O'Hara becomes wealthy, she establishes a lumber factory. A man walks in, followed by dozens of prisoners, looking filthy and dejected, dressed in humiliating prison outfits and shuffling in chains.

---

[1] Professor Hadar Aviram holds the Harry and Lillian Hastings Research Chair at UC Hastings College of the Law, where she teaches and writes about criminal justice and civil rights. Her work lies at the crossroads of law, criminology, and public policy, and encompasses quantitative, qualitative, and experimental research. Prof. Aviram's book *Cheap on Crime: Recession-Era Politics and the Transformation of American Punishment* examines the impact of the 2008 financial crisis on the American correctional landscape. She is the current President of the Western Society of Criminology, a frequent commentator on criminal justice and politics in the media, and the owner of the California Correctional Crisis blog.

[2] Margaret Mitchell, *Gone With the Wind* (New York: Macmillan, 1936).

[3] *Gone with the Wind*, directed by Victor Fleming (1939, Culver City, CA: Selznick International Pictures), film.

Scarlett negotiates with the owner of the chain gang for their services as workers in the factory, and later vociferously defends her decision to hire them to Ashley.

What might be surprising to modern viewers is that all the chain gang inmates are white. Indeed, during the course of the Civil War, disciplinary transgressions by slaves were addressed by their masters, and the criminal justice system's engagement with slaves was infrequent and inconsistent. But this picture had completely transformed within a decade of the civil war: the racial composition of prisons had completely changed, and minority populations, particularly African Americans and Latinos, had come to be overrepresented in the criminal justice system. The abolition of slavery, with the repeal of forced labor and the Thirteenth Amendment, was made with an important exception: forced labor would be allowed in prisons.[4] By the time Mitchell wrote her novel and Selznick produced its cinematic adaptation, chain gangs were composed of predominantly African-American prisoners, who were made to work in conditions remarkably similar to those of their ancestors in slavery and governed by standards similar to those that had governed slavery regimes.[5]

This overrepresentation persists to this day. The Pew Center on the States issued two reports examining the size and characteristics of the prison population, finding alarming overrepresentation of minorities. Intersecting age and gender with race yields even more extreme disparities: one in nine black men aged 18-24 is in prison, and one in three is under some form of correctional supervision (incarcerated, on probation or on parole). As Loïc Wacquant explains, hyperincarceration is the last phase in a series of institutional and social constructions designed to perpetuate,

---

[4] Michelle Alexander, *The New Jim Crow: Mass Incarceration in the Age of Colorblindness* (New York: The New Press, 2010).

[5] Alex Reinert, "Reconceptualizing the Eighth Amendment: Slaves, Prisoners, and 'Cruel and Unusual' Punishment," *North Carolina Law Review 94*, (2016): 817-860; Cardozo Legal Studies Research Paper No. 484 (April 2016), accessed https://ssrn.com/abstract=2758342.

and even deepen, racial domination and inequality.⁶ How do so many members of racial minorities end up incarcerated? Are our prisons the natural successors of slavery, the Southern Jim Crow regime, and the Northern urban ghetto?

To understand this trajectory, this short article follows the chronology of the criminal process, identifying institutional factors that contribute to the racial imbalance in the prison population. Finally, we discuss some implications of racial disparities.

Do People of Color Commit More Crime?

A possible benign explanation for racial disparity in prison is that people of color commit more crime, and thus are overrepresented in prison. As Elizabeth Hinton shows in her recent book *From the War on Poverty to the War on Crime*, this hypothesis dominated the conversation about crime in the 1960s. Long before Richard Nixon made inner-city crime the centerpiece of his presidential campaign, both the Kennedy and Johnson administrations were preoccupied with crime specifically as a minority phenomenon.⁷ The welfarist criminologists of that era, such as Richard Cloward and Lloyd Ohlin, attributed crime to the differential opportunities available to people of working class backgrounds, theorizing that people to whom fewer legitimate opportunities were presented would recur to illegitimate ones.⁸ In this vein, President Johnson's National Criminal Justice Commission's report focused on the pathology of the black family and on disorganized, vulnerable neighborhoods as the causes of

---

6   Loïc Wacquant, "From Slavery to Mass Incarceration: Rethinking the 'Race Question' in the US," *New Left Review* 13, (2002): 55-56.

7   Elizabeth Hinton, *From the War on Poverty to the War on Crime* (Cambridge, MA: Harvard University Press, 2016).

8   Richard A. Cloward and Lloyd E. Ohlin, *Delinquency and Opportunity: A Study of Delinquent Gangs* (New York: The Free Press, 1966).

crime.[9] The solutions advocated by the administration included top-down interventions that ignored existing good role models within the neighborhoods and sought to address the deficiencies in inner-city communities through top-down welfare interventions from the outside. These well-intentioned policies contributed to the notion that crime was, essentially, a Black and Latino problem. As Kahlil Gibran Muhammad explains in *The Condemnation of Blackness*, this perspective reflected opinions that were prevalent in the urban North, where the early 20th century saw distinctions drawn between African Americans and other, supposedly noncriminal, minorities.[10]

In this respect, President Nixon's reliance on crime control as a proxy for racialized policy was not much of a dramatic departure from his predecessors. Nixon's presidential campaign was thus not the first time that crime was made into a national issue, but it was notable for highlighting the rising crime rates and promising to curb the Warren Court's coddling of suspects and defendants. These promises were not premised on lies: FBI crime statistics at the time did register a rise in crime, particularly in violent crime. However, as Katherine Beckett shows in *Making Crime Pay* public fear of crime was more a response to political rhetoric than to actual crime. Moreover, the increase in crime was likely not as sharp as the data suggests, because until the mid-1970s crime reporting to the FBI was only partial.[11] Nixon's first term was characterized by a significant infusion of federal funds into municipal police departments, which led to an increase in arrests.[12]

---

[9] *The Challenge of Crime in A Free Society*, Report By the President's Commission on Law Enforcement and Administration of Justice (Washington, D.C.: United States Government Printing Office, February 1967).

[10] Khalil Gibran Muhammad, *The Condemnation of Blackness: Race, Crime, and the Making of Modern Urban America* (Cambridge, MA: Harvard University Press, 2010).

[11] Katherine Beckett, *Making Crime Pay* (Oxford: Oxford University Press, 1967).

[12] Hadar Aviram, *Cheap on Crime: Recession-Era Politics and the Transformation of American Punishment* (Oakland, CA: University of California Press, 2015) and Elizabeth Hinton, *From the War on Poverty to the War on Crime: The Making of Masss Incarceration in America* (Harvard University Press, 2016).

In his second term, he adopted a more aggressive position toward drugs, enhancing federal enforcement and incentivizing enforcement on the state level.[13] As a top Nixon aide admitted years later, these policies were specifically designed to target minorities, especially African Americans.[14]

Before discussing the impact of differential law enforcement on racial disparities, it is important to offer a caveat: by contrast to some perceptions, nonviolent drug offenders constitute no more than a fifth of the state and federal prison population. While racial disparities in nonviolent drug arrests can be easily attributable to differential law enforcement strategies in different neighborhoods, racial disparities in violent crime cannot be explained away that easily. In his examination of racial critiques of mass incarceration, James Formanreminds us that the tendency to attribute racial disparities in criminal justice to the war on drugs can explain only part of the disparities, and that crime rates can account for the gaps in violent crime.[15] Jill Leovy, author of *Ghettoside* reminds us also that, in our focus on over-enforcement in inner-city neighborhoods, we tend to de-emphasize investigating and solving violent crime in the same neighborhoods, where not only the perpetrators, but also the victims, tend to be poor people of color.[16]

It is important to keep in mind that not all categories of violent crime receive the same type of police attention, or even come to the attention of the police. For example, domestic violence and interpersonal abuse between friends and family members tends to be

---

[13] Jonathan Simon, *Governing Through Crime: How the War on Crime Transformed American Democracy and Created a Culture of Fear* (New York: Oxford University Press, 2007).

[14] Dan Baum, "Legalize It All: How to Win the War on Drugs," *Harpers Magazine* (April 2016), accessed https://harpers.org/archive/2016/04/legalize-it-all/.

[15] James Forman Jr., "Racial Critiques of Mass Incarceration: Beyond the New Jim Crow," *Yale Law School: Faculty Scholarship Series*, Paper 3599 (2012), accessed http://digitalcommons.law.yale.edu/cgi/viewcontent.cgi?article=4599&context=fss_papers.

[16] Jill Leovy, *Ghettoside: A True Story of Murder in America* (Spiegel and Grau: Reprint Edition, 2015).

severely underreported to the police and may skew our perspectives on violent behavior. But even agreeing that the gap in punishment for violent offenses reflects, at least partly, different rates of this behavior, the incidence of violent crimes in settings where poverty and lack of opportunity have given rise to behavioral codes that invite such behavior. In *Listening to Killers*, James Garbarini mentions that some causes of crime that appear "insane" to people who live relatively calm and secure middle-class existences make perfect sense to someone who lives in an environment of constant violence and trauma.[17] Violent crime under such circumstances cannot be attributed to racial differences if the nexus between urban spatial segregation and environmental deprivation is ignored.

For less serious categories of crime, however, law enforcement strategies and police discretion make a difference. We now turn to those.

Policing and Race: Explicit, Implicit, and Systemic Biases

Police officers have a considerable degree of discretion in enforcing the law, and this discretion is, unfortunately, sometimes applied in ways that are discriminatory toward people of color.[18] While, undoubtedly, some officers harbor racialized stereotypes (the recent texting scandal at the San Francisco police department is a grim reminder), for many officers racial biases are subconscious and implicit. Nikki Joneshas studied camera footage of police-citizen encounters and conducted interviews with police officers and suspects, and has found that many

---

[17] James Garbarini, *Listening to Killers: Lessons Learned from My Twenty Years as a Psychological Expert Witness in Murder Cases* (Oakland, CA: University of California Press, 2015).

[18] Joseph Goldstein, "Police Discretion Not to Invoke the Criminal Process: Low-Visibility Decisions in the Administration of Justice Joseph Goldstein," *Yale Law School: Faculty Scholarship Series* 69, no. 4, paper 2426 (1960), accessed http://digitalcommons.law.yale.edu/cgi/viewcontent.cgi?article=3417&context=fss_papers.

of the characteristics that make police officers concerned a own safety are also stereotypical markers of racial identity.[19] Ironically, as L. Song Richardson found, the more concerned the police officer is that his or her behavior will be interpreted as racist, the more likely they are to escalate a conflict with a citizen.[20] Indeed, Frank Zimring's recent analysis of lethal police force reveals that African Americans are twice as likely to be victims of a shooting than their percentage in the population.[21]

But some racial differences in enforcement stem not from individual officers' decisionmaking but from institutional priorities. Chuck Epp, Steve Maynard-Moody and Donald Haider-Markel's study of car stops was based on thousands of interviews with car drivers in the Kansas metropolitan area.[22] Epp et al. found that the drivers reported two types of stops: an ordinary traffic stop, justifiably related to a violation of the traffic code and ending in a warning or a citation, and an "investigatory stop," triggered by an insignificant violation and aimed at obtaining consent or suspicion against the driver. The latter category was employed, for the most part, with African American drivers, and its consequences could range from mere inconvenience to a formal arrest. The prevalence of these stops, and the drivers' awareness that the police officers were merely "fishing" for a drug violation, contributed to the sense of disillusionment and mistrust in the police—even if the individual police officers were courteous. Moreover, because investigative stops are designed as "fishing

---

[19] Nikki Jones, "How Things Fall Apart: Race and Suspicion in Police-Civilian Encounters," ensemble video 01:16:49, *Clarke Forum for Contemporary Issues: Public Lectures* (October 28, 2015), accessed https://ensemble.dickinson.edu/Watch/GwjkqME_nk-cfrc421yRTw.

[20] L. Song Richardson, "Police Racial Violence: Lessons from Social Psychology," *Fordham Law Review*, forthcoming; UC Irvine School of Law, no. 72 (August 2015), accessed https://papers.ssrn.com/sol3/papers.cfm?abstract_id=2641114.

[21] Franklin Zimring, *When Police Kill* (Harvard University Press, 2017).

[22] Charles R. Epp, Seven Maynard-Moody, and Donald P. Haider-Markel, *Pulled Over: How Police Stops Define Race and Citizenship* (University of Chicago Press Books, 2014).

expeditions" from their very beginning, the pattern revealed by the interviews suggested a systematic policy of stopping African American drivers, beyond the explicit or implicit biases of the individual police officers.

Systemic policing disparities can be noted in other ways as well. This is especially true for police use of stop-and-frisk (a brief detention accompanied by a pat-down of the suspects' outer clothes) in so-called high-crime neighborhoods. This practice was recognized as constitutional in Terry v. Ohio and extensively utilized in inner city areas, mostly against people of color.[23] The landmark decision in Floyd v. City of New York, which severely curbed the use of stop-and-frisk in New York City, was based on a report by Jeffrey Fagan, which found that many street detentions were unconstitutional in that they lacked individualized suspicion, and those that were based on suspicion framed it very vaguely.[24] Fagan found that most stops happened in Black and Latino neighborhoods, even after adjusting for crime rates, social conditions, and allocation of police resources.[25] In the few cases in which contraband is actually found on the detained person, Black and Latino suspects were shown to be arrested more frequently than White suspects.

While car stops and stop-and-frisk practices almost never yield evidence that leads to incarceration, they are deployed against minority populations at a frequency that likely affects detention and incarceration rates. Moreover, even in the cases in which no evidence is found and no one is incarcerated, the deployment of these techniques confirms and calcifies racial stereotypes and breeds an atmosphere of suspicion and mistrust between the police and the communities they serve, which eventually works to the detriment of these communities.

---

[23] Terry v. Ohio, 392 U.S. 79, 88 S. Ct. 1868, 20 L. Ed. 2d 889 (1968).
[24] Jeffrey Fagan, et al., "Street Stops and Broken Windows Revisited: Race and Order Maintenance Policing in a Safe and Changing City," Exploring Race, Ethnicity and Policing: Essential Readings 309 (New York University Press, 2010).
[25] Floyd v. City of New York, 813 F. Supp. 2d 417 S.D.N.Y. (2011).

How Race Operates in the Criminal Courtroom

In his book *Locked In*, John Pfaff attributes the mass incarceration crisis to charging decisions by county prosecutors.[26] Prosecutors have vast discretion in charging and, according to Pfaff, the tendency to overcharge, especially in violent offense cases, is the determining factor in increasing incarceration. Since racial disparities are present in this category, what contributes to an increase in the prison population as a whole also maintains racial disparities. Pfaff, as well as Christopher Seeds, argue that the Obama-era policies to reduce incarceration have, for the most part, targeted nonviolent offenders, while retrenching public opinion about, and justification of, punishment for violent offenders.[27] But the category of people charged with violent felonies is not a monolith, and prosecutors have considerable leeway in deciding on the quantity and the severity of charges.

In 1996, the Supreme Court was required to weigh in on a direct challenge to prosecutorial discretion.[28] Christopher Armstrong, charged with possession of crack cocaine, filed a motion for discovery, claiming that black defendants are disproportionately prosecuted for possession of crack cocaine. The Supreme Court rejected Armstrong's claims, stating that defendants who wish to make discrimination claims must show that similarly situated suspects of other races were not prosecuted, and that the data provided by Armstrong did not suffice to show such a claim. This outcome is ironic in light of the fact that Armstrong sought to obtain information, via discovery, that might have enabled him to make such claims.

At the initial charging phase, the court also decides on pretrial release conditions. Studies of bail and detention reveal that

---

[26] John F. Pfaff, *Locked In: The True Causes of Mass Incarceration and How to Achieve Real Reform* (New York: Basic Books, 2017).

[27] Christopher Seeds, *Bifurcation Nation: Strategy in Contemporary American Punishment* (New York: New York University, 2015), accessed https://papers.ssrn.com/sol3/papers.cfm?abstract_id=2613083.

[28] United States v. Armstrong, 517 U.S. 456, 116 S. Ct. 1480, 134 L. Ed. 2d 687 (1996).

defendants of color are disproportionately held before trial, but at least in one study, this disparity disappeared when controlling for severity of the offense.[29] Since many counties rely on bail schedules for assessing amount of bail, it makes sense that this initial decision would be racially neutral. However, the actual outcome of a bail decision depends not only on the judge's determination, but also on the defendant's ability to pay. To the extent that race intersects with class, inability to pay a bail bondsman plays an important part in dooming some people to pretrial detention, which later harms their chances at trial by increasing the stress level on them and their families and depriving them of an opportunity to freely consult with a defense attorney and organize their defense. The recent tragic suicide of Kaleef Browder, held in jail for lengthy periods of time under deplorable conditions, is a grim reminder of the destructive effects of pretrial detention.

Scholars of lower criminal courts have observed stark racial disparities in criminal courtrooms. As early as the 1970s, Malcolm Feeleycommented on such disparities, arguing that the routinized and repetitive work of criminal courtrooms numbs the professionals to the circumstances of those less fortunate than them.[30] In her book *Crook County*, Nicole Gonzalez Van Cleve goes farther by suggesting that institutional racism permeates the work and dynamic of the criminal court in Chicago.[31] She notes the two lines at the entrance of the court: the almost-all-white line of professionals ushered in and the long, almost-all-black-and-brown line of defendants and victims coming in. She shows the disregard, off-color jokes, and mocking use of ebonics in conversation about criminal defendants,

---

[29] Frank McIntyre and Shima Baradaran, "Race, Prediction, and Pretrial Detention," Journal of Empirical Legal Studies 10, no. 4 (December 2013): 741-770, accessed http://onlinelibrary.wiley.com/doi/10.1111/jels.12026/full.

[30] Malcolm M. Feeley, *The Process Is the Punishment: Handling Cases in a Lower Criminal Court* (New York: Russell Sage Foundation, 1992).

[31] Nicole Gonzalez van Cleve, *Crook County: Racism and Injustice in America's Largest Criminal Court* (Stanford, CA: Stanford University Press, 2016).

and demonstrates how some people's cultural backgrounds lead to them classifying others as "mops" undeserving of compassion or opportunities. An environment rife with stereotypes and plagued by empathy fatigue invites negative interpretations of people's motives and actions, which may well factor into decisions to incarcerate.

Trial Outcomes: Convictions and Sentences

It is a sad testament to the power of race in decision making that jury selection proceedings are intensely racialized. Indeed, numerous Supreme Court decisions parse out the circumstances in which prospective jurors can be asked whether they harbor racial biases. Naturally, such questioning cannot weed out implicit biases, which is why the parties often recur to peremptory challenges in an effort to excuse prospective jurors that might be hostile to their side because of their race. In Batson v. Kentucky, the Supreme Court decided that a pattern of jury strikes that suggests a racial motive is constitutionally impermissible.[32] Recently, in Foster v. Chatman, the Court learned of the racial pattern behind jury strikes from the prosecutors' notes, which included notations about jurors' race in them.[33]

These "games" of race-based jury exclusion persist because the lawyers are right in their assumption of biases: studies in social psychology confirm that trial outcomes are tied to jurors' races. In a mock-jury experiment, Craig Haney and Mona Lynch presented jury panels with a homicide case, randomly assigning racial identities to the defendant and the victim.[34] They found that juries with a higher concentration of white male jurors were more likely to vote for the death penalty in cases involving black defendants.

---

[32] Batson v. Kentucky, 476 U.S. 79, 106 S. Ct. 1712, 90 L. Ed. 2d 69 (1986).
[33] Foster v. Chatman, No. 14-8349, 578 U.S. S. Ct.7 (2016).
[34] Mona Lynch and Craig Haney, "Looking Across the Empathic Divide: Racialized Decisions Making on the Capital Jury," Michigan State Law Review 2011, no.2012-63 (2011): 753, accessed https://ssrn.com/abstract=2091956

Such biases are not unique to lay jurors. As Cassia Spohn shows in her book *How Do Judges Decide?* professional judges are also informed by their own demographic characteristics and experiences, which may involve implicit or explicit biases.[35] Interestingly, racial bias is not only related to the race of the defendant, but also to the race of the victim. In a famous study, David Baldus found that the death penalty was more likely to be applied in homicide cases involving a white victim.[36] The convicted defendant in Mcleskey v. Kemp tried to rely on Baldus' study to argue that the death penalty is imposed in a discriminatory manner, but without success.[37] The Supreme Court stated that, in order to prove discrimination, the petitioner would have to show how racial animus played a role in his or her particular case. This would, of course, be difficult to show, partly because racial biases are often implicit, and partly because patterns of discrimination are easier to discover in the aggregate.

But in many cases, trial outcome disparities stem not from the discretion of judges and juries, but from the law itself. Starting in the late 1970s, the federal government and the states shifted from an indeterminate sentencing system, which afforded broad discretion to judges, to a determinate system, in which sentences are set according to the severity of the offense and the defendant's criminal history, either by a sentencing commission or by the legislature. While the law applies universally, it often embeds racism into seemingly neutral sections. A classic example is the Controlled Substances Act's sentencing for different types of drugs. Until recently, the sentence for offenses involving crack cocaine, which is primarily associated with African American users and sellers, was a hundred times harsher than the sentence for identical offenses involving powder cocaine, associated more closely with white users. The disparity was not

---

[35] Cassia C. Spohn, *How Do Judges Decide? The Search for Fairness and Justice in Punishment* (SAGE Publications, Inc., 2009).

[36] David C. Baldus, *Statistical Proof of Discrimination* (Colorado Springs: Shepard's Inc., 1980).

[37] McCleskey v. Kemp, 22 Ill.481 U.S. 279, 107 S. Ct. 1756, 95 L. Ed. 2d 262 (1987).

justified by considerably greater danger or addictiveness of the former drug compared to the latter, and it was only decades later, during the Obama administration, that the disparity was reduced to an eighteen-to-one ratio. The Obama administration also noted the effect of harsh mandatory minimums on the African American community and worked to reduce the destructive effects of federal drug sentencing partly for reasons of racial equality.

Conclusions and Implications

The overview above offers substantiation for the claim that racial disparities in incarceration stem from racialized assumptions and practices that precede the incarceration stage: social disadvantage that produces violent crime; discriminatory policing practices; extensive prosecutorial discretion, which is very resistant to judicial review; the everyday realities of lower courtroom practices; and the impact of race, and other demographic factors that intersect with it, on sentencing. The end product is disturbing: a prison population that is black and brown beyond the representation of these groups in the population, governed and locked up by state professional machinations that are largely white.

The overrepresentation of racial minorities in prison matters not only because of the trauma of incarceration itself, but also because of the impact of incarceration on a person's life after release. For formerly incarcerated people, adjusting to life on the outside with a criminal record that hinders their ability to obtain housing, employment, and education, is a real liability. That these hurdles disproportionately affect members of racial minority groups is extremely problematic. Incarceration also carries the civic penalty of temporary or permanent disenfranchisement, and its imbalanced effect on minority populations means that these populations are disproportionately deprived of civic participation in their communities.

The Spatial Information Design Lab (SIDL) has mapped "million dollar blocks": entire blocks whose inhabitants are incarcerated to the tune of at least a million dollars.[38] The spatial distribution of these blocks is, of course, not random; they are concentrated in low-income, minority neighborhoods. As a result, entire communities are deprived of their members, and generations of children grow up in environments that normalize mass incarceration as an inescapable fact of life. This is a phenomenon we must fight by unseating the causes of differential crime as well as differential criminalization: poverty, deprivation, institutional racism, white supremacy, and lack of empathy for the "other."

---

[38] Laura Kurgan and Eric Cadora, "Million Dollar Blocks," *Spatial Information Design Lab: Center for Spatial Research, Columbia University*, accessed http://spatialinformationdesignlab.org/projects.php %3Fid%3D16.

Where You Can't Be Colorblind: Race, Incarceration, and Reentry

KIMBERLY RICHMAN[1]

As a criminal, you have scarcely more rights, and arguably less respect, than a black man living in Alabama at the height of Jim Crow. We have not ended racial caste in America; we have merely redesigned it."
— Michelle Alexander, *The New Jim Crow*

The impact of both race and socio-economic status on criminal justice outcomes at every step of the process from arrest to sentencing has been well documented, and is no longer a surprise to the undergraduate students who have taken my Criminology courses. Less frequently considered, however, are the many ways that race and incarceration

---

[1] Kimberly Richman, PhD, is a Professor of Sociology and Legal Studies at the University of San Francisco, where she was named a Dean's Scholar in 2016. She has published two-award winning books with New York University Press, and numerous book chapters and journal articles. Her current research examines the lived experiences of punishment and rehabilitation as defined by incarcerated men at varying security levels in the state of Ohio. Additionally, she is a past President of the Western Society of Criminology and sits on the Board of Directors of two Bay Area nonprofits working with incarcerated and formerly incarcerated individuals. She has 13 years of experience running programs in San Quentin State Prison and co-founded the nonprofit Alliance for CHANGE, which works with incarcerated men pre- and post- release to assist with successful reintegration.

interface post-conviction. After all, the individuals whose cases make the evening news upon arrest and trial are largely forgotten once they are securely locked behind prison walls. Fictionalized accounts do give the public a sense of the racially charged places that prisons are, but without a sense of the nuance and variation that characterize this relationship in real life, let alone what happens when the long-forgotten prisoner returns to society. In what follows, I examine the interplay of race and incarceration in three settings: first, in prison life including intake, housing, and gangs; next, in prison rehabilitative programs; and finally, in the process of re-entering society after incarceration.[2]

The 13th Amendment, Prison Gangs, and the Hyper-Racialized World of Prison

Certainly the racial cliques and gangs of prison TV shows are not all fiction. There is a long well-documented history of de facto and institutionalized racial segregation in U.S. prisons, a practice that continues today. This is not an accident: as Michelle Alexander and others have pointed out painstakingly, the 13th Amendment did not end slavery. Amy Smith and R. Malik Harris show that after the Civil War, the law transitioned to "make way for a new type of slavery… woven into the language of the 13th Amendment [which] would prove more durable than the institution of slavery." Slave labor was replaced by convict leasing, and Southern prisons began filling up with Black Americans at a rapid pace. In short, prisons became the new plantations, complete with peonage, financial interests, and racial segregation.

Until very recently, this racial segregation was reflected in institutional housing policy, created at the state level, whereby prisoners were automatically housed with members of their own race. The 21st-century rationale given was to reduce friction and violence, particularly that associated with race-based prison gangs. Prison gangs were, and remain,

---

[2] My comments and observations are based primarily on men's prisons, though the section on reentry applies to all formerly incarcerated people.

a persistent and severe source of violence and conflict, and thus often do affect many aspects of prison operations.[3] When it became no longer palatable for the state to call race-based housing and segregation what it was, gang membership became a proxy for race. Most prison gangs are race-based, and gang membership factors into the racial identity claimed by prisoners upon intake. Racial and gang divisions brought in from the streets are exacerbated by the overwhelming pressure to align oneself with a racial gang—such as the largely Latino Norteños (Nuestra Familia) and Sureños (Mexican Mafia), the white Aryan Brotherhood and Nazi Low Riders, or the largely African American Bloods and Crips—to secure personal protection. Racial/gang segregation was, and still is to a degree, justified as a safety measure.

Once the U.S. Supreme Court overturned racially segregated housing in prisons in the 2005 U. S. Supreme Court case *Johnson v. California* (543 U.S. 499), California continued to group people according to race under the auspices of safety—including enforcing racialized lockdowns after riots in the prison—until that too was ended in California by a legal settlement in 2014.[4] Still, this hyper-racialization continued, in part through a set of interactions normally taking place during prisoners' intake. Correctional officers solicit the individuals' racial and gang self-identification, but also limit their available choices and sometimes impose a racial identity that the prisoner does not claim for him or herself. Prisons typically classify prisoners into one of four racial categories: Black, White, Mexican, or Other.[5] There is no option for claiming a bi-racial or multi-racial

---

[3] It is also important to note the primary function of prison gangs: controlling the drug trade, a function that is inextricably connected to the racialized War on Drugs.

[4] This is the practice of indefinitely locking in their cell, or in a solitary confinement cell, all members of the race or races involved in the riot.

[5] "Other" is the classification given to Asian and Pacific Islanders, Native Americans or other indigenous groups, and Middle Easterners. The term "Mexican" is used to refer to all people of Latino/a descent, including both South and Central Americans. In some prison systems, the category of "Other" is left out entirely, leaving these ethnicities to choose from one of the remaining three categories.

status, or declining to declare a race.[6] As social theorist Loïc Wacquant has written, these practices make prison the "main machine for 'race making'." Indeed, these dynamics force prisoners into a time warp society, with far more explicitly spoken and enforced racism than is, at least outwardly, acceptable in 21st-century America. One enters a prison and is thrown back into a world where Caucasians and African Americans do not eat at the same tables or drink from the same water fountains. If this is not moderated or mitigated by other factors, it can be a severe impediment to rehabilitation and reentry, as well as an affront to social justice.

Breaking the Chains: Rehabilitation as Integration

Although the specific populations vary, many features of this racial system are ubiquitous across prisons. However, they are not universal. It is in lower security prison settings, what would generally be called Level II or Level I facilities, that one typically sees the most variation from the norms of racial segregation and prison gangs. There are a number of reasons for this, but foremost among them is the availability of vocational, educational, and self-help programs. When prisoners in higher security prisons are able to stay violence-free for a long enough time, they are often transferred to a lower security prison. In these "mainline" populations, the incarcerated men or women are usually assigned to either work, classes, or a rehabilitative program of some sort. In this setting, racial segregation and racial politics are disrupted and mitigated by these programs, which necessarily force together prisoners of different races and backgrounds into a task-focused or therapeutic setting.

---

[6] However, it is important to note that often what is sought by officers in these interactions is not simply a race as marked by one's appearance, but an identification with a particular group for the purposes of housing. In other words, in prison vernacular, it matters less what your ethnicity and heredity are, and more who you choose to "run with" (associate with, engage in crime or gang activity with, and seek protection from).

Scholars and prison program providers have provided a number of accounts of this usually latent effect of these programs and jobs. Goodman examines the minimum security fire camps, located outside of prison walls, as a setting where the normal racial strictures of prison are notably limited. Prisoners who satisfy certain requirements—have few years left in their sentence, are not presently gang affiliated, and do not have certain conviction offenses—can be endorsed to go to one of these camps, where they undergo rigorous training to fight wildfires. The setting is much smaller and less restrictive than the prison. Here, there is very much a sense of camaraderie and mutual support "on the line"—at the site of a wildfire—where racial segregation and distinctions fall away, and workers are united against a common threat: fire. There is general consensus that while working, there is no place for racial segregation. While in some cases segregation may still occur in the housing and dining areas of the fire camps, it is nowhere near as strictly enforced as in walled and higher security prisons. Thus, while racial distinctions still may exist at some level, they are not tinged with violence, and they are seen as malleable. In a similar way, competitive group sports in prison also unify prisoners of different races with a common goal and external "enemy," or competitor.

Another setting that can set the stage for racial integration is within the religious communities of the prison. While some states' prison systems only offer Judeo-Christian services, those in California house a surprising array of faith traditions: Catholic, Protestant, Jewish, Muslim, Wiccan, Mormon, Buddhist, and Norse, to name just a few. Like the firehouse and sports field, these worship spaces are, for the most part, explicitly racially integrated, uniting participants in an identification and practice outside of the confines of the prison's racial categories.[7] Arguably, the cross-racial bonds formed within

---

[7] Some, such as the Muslim community and the Mormon community, are more heavily populated by a particular race because of the communities from which they derive, but they are not exclusive to that race. Others—in particular the Wiccan and Norse religious groups—are traditionally not as inclusive because of their frequent association with white supremacist groups.

the various chapels' programs (or in some prisons, the "Interfaith Chapel") are among the strongest outside of prison gangs, because the participants' faith is central to their being and, in some cases, to their rehabilitation. Some prisoners come to find eventually that they have more in common with others in the faith community—or even those of other faith traditions—than they do with members of their own race who continue to engage in violent or gang activity. A Jew and a Muslim using a common prayer facility are united in their common goals of worship and observance more than either is to any given member of their race who is not practicing—or is explicitly contradicting—their faith traditions.

My own experience volunteering and running programs in San Quentin State Prison has allowed me insight into the unique features of other prison programs that similarly further the project of blunting the hyper-racialized prison environment. In 2008, I co-founded, along with a handful of incarcerated men and other community volunteers, a non-profit prison program called the Alliance for CHANGE. While most self-help programs in prison go to great lengths to emphasize individualism in order to teach accountability, without any regard for larger social structures, the Alliance sought to bring a more distinctly sociological awareness to its participants. We created an 18-week social justice-based curriculum, which taught members about models of justice ranging from retributive justice to restorative, community, and even transformative justice, in an immersive and interactive setting. The goal is to help participants understand their place in a diverse community and to examine how race, class, and gender have impacted them and their communities. Participants also learn how recognizing and combatting these axes of oppression can help them build a more just society. We make an effort to diversify each class of 20 participants as much as possible.

What happens next among the participants ranges from resistance, to grudging acceptance, to epiphany. From the first week of class, students are forced to take on gender, race and class identities in role-play situations that may be dramatically distinct from their own. In one exercise in the pilot class, a Caucasian man with casual ties to white supremacist prison gangs was asked to embody the role of a poor Black elderly woman—and was paired, in this role, with a middle-class African American classmate. In other parts of the class, participants learn about broader social systems of oppression, as well as local policies and practices, which produce and reinforce the cycle of poverty in which many of them grew up. A pinnacle of the experience is a mock trial in which plaintiff and defense teams are composed of mixed race groups. At the end of the eighteen-week curriculum, participants are prepared to work together to formulate solutions to crime and other community problems that do not rely on incarceration—in other words, to make prisons obsolete.

Evaluations, observations, and testimonials from participants reveal a deeply impactful process that calls into question and critically examines many of the racial and gendered practices and ideologies that have governed their lives while incarcerated. It also challenges pre-prison beliefs about group identities, structural forces and systemic inequalities, and offers models of collaboration and reconciliation that can be taken back to their communities upon their release. Importantly, these models of collaboration and reconciliation do not have to wait for parole. Participants immediately begin to look for their application within their prison community.

One anecdote demonstrates the impact of the program particularly well. Alliance graduation ceremonies confer completion certificates according to a unique tradition. Rather than an instructor or program leader conferring the certificates in a top-down manner, each participant stands in turn to confer the certificate upon the participant next to him, and introduces the recipient with a few words of appreciation for what he contributed to the class. I will never forget the graduation in which a white supremacist former "shot caller,"[8] replete with Aryan Brotherhood tattoos, sat next to an elderly African American man with long dreadlocks. As the white participant rose

---

[8] "Shot caller" is the term used for the leaders of the various prison gangs and racial groups.

to present the certificate to the classmate next to him, he stated that he never imagined he would be in a classroom presenting a certificate to "a black guy." He then went on to give his appreciation for the gentleman, and all he had learned from him over the course of the last five months. When the African American man rose to claim his certificate, the Caucasian student embraced him in a hug, and the two continued to hug for several more seconds. When he released from the embrace, the former white supremacist stated to the class, with tears in his eyes, "That's the first time in my life I ever hugged a black man."

The Challenges of Race and Reentry

Providers of such programs hope that, in addition to breaking down or at least muting some of the conflicts and barriers erected in prison, they prepare participants for a productive and crime-free life once they leave prison. In California, release from prison happens in two different ways. Since 1977, most people convicted of crimes are sentenced to a set term in prison that is pre-determined upon their conviction. In other words, they will serve, for example, ten years and then be released, no matter what (unless they have committed more crimes while incarcerated). This is what is called *determinate* sentencing. The sentencing scheme that existed prior to this, and is in limited usage today, is called *indeterminate* sentencing. Under indeterminate sentencing, those convicted of a crime are given a range of years to serve, typically something like seven years to life or fifteen years to life. To determine their actual release date, the person was required to appear in front of a parole board whose job it is to determine whether they continue to pose a threat to society. This system only applies to a small handful of those convicted: those convicted of murder, attempted murder, or kidnapping; those serving twenty-five years to life under the Three Strikes Law; and those sentenced under certain enhancement laws, such as the 10-20-Life gun law.⁹ Only those whose release date depends on a parole board determination have a built-in incentive to participate in rehabilitative programs. This, in turn, has a dramatic effect on their process of reentry into the community upon parole.

In general, this latter group is better prepared for reintegration into society. They have been incentivized to participate in rehabilitative and educational programs when available, and to learn vocational trades. They have been put through the grueling and extremely selective process of convincing a parole board composed of former law enforcement personnel that they are deserving of release.¹⁰ Consequently, this population—the "lifers" as they are called—have the lowest recidivism rates. That is, they are the least likely of anyone released from prison to return to prison within three years. In fact, not a single person convicted of murder and subsequently paroled in California has, in the modern era for which there are statistics, gone on to commit another murder. However, this surprising success rate

---

[9] Although this group represents a minority of overall criminal convictions, they today represent a larger proportion of those in prison in California than in the past—of 130,000 currently incarcerated in state prison, 34,000 have indeterminate life sentences. This is due to California's Realignment policy, which since 2012 sends those with lesser convictions and parole violations to county jail rather than state prison, as well as Prop 47, which re-designated certain low-level felonies as misdemeanors.

[10] Even parole board decision-making is in some cases racially influenced. In one recent case shared by a prisoner's attorney, an individual born in Mexico but serving time in California was denied parole because he could not prove he had an acceptably complete parole plan to implement once he was deported back to Mexico upon his release. In other words, he was expected to have located a halfway house or other residential facility, a job, and a relapse prevention system in Mexico (where these things might or might not exist), even though as a prisoner he was not allowed to communicate with anyone in Mexico or access the internet to research programs there. In this sense, even being found suitable for parole requires a certain amount of cultural and social capital that those already on the margins are less likely to have.

obscures the many difficulties endemic to the reentry process, which affect some racial and class demographics more heavily than others.

The population of former prisoners reentering free society has expanded considerably since the crisis of mass incarceration and unconstitutional overcrowding was explicitly and legally acknowledged in the early 2010s. Not surprisingly this reentry population is disproportionately minority—reflecting the observation by Alexander, Thompson and others that ours was less a *mass* incarceration equally distributed across the population, and more a *hyper*-incarceration, at extreme rates, localized in specific communities of color. By and large, the community that one is arrested in is the community to which one is released. That means that the communities disproportionately affected by racial profiling and other police strategies, by the War on Drugs, and by hyper-incarceration, are the very same ones that must receive the majority of paroled prisoners upon their release. Not only are the communities, whose members are already impoverished, not prepared to support this influx of formerly incarcerated men and women, but the parolees themselves—mostly having served determinate sentences—are woefully underprepared. This creates a vicious cycle in which the individuals coming out of prison, having received no meaningful rehabilitation or preparation for release, are more likely to commit another crime, and the community is again less safe and further impacted by their re-incarceration.

There is abundant empirical research that shows how African American and Latinx ex-offenders are disadvantaged in the reentry process. The two most important ingredients of successful reentry are housing and employment. Ironically, it is in these two venues where rampant discrimination persists. In one important study, Devah Pager sent matched samples of job seekers, half black and half white, one with a purported criminal record and one with no criminal record, to apply for various jobs. Each job seeker had an identical profile other than these two characteristics. She found that Blacks in each category were half as likely as their White counterparts to be offered jobs, and even Black applicants with *no prior criminal record* were less likely than white applicants *with* a criminal record to be hired. This finding has been corroborated by subsequent research, which also found that Latino ex-offenders were similarly unlikely to be hired.

Likewise, research indicates that the availability of post-release housing is dually affected by conviction status and race. The 1990 Anti-Drug Abuse Act and the 1996 HUD "One Strike" Initiative included provisions which required public housing authorities to screen out or remove any tenants who "engaged in criminal activity, including drug-related criminal activity," and instituted a lifetime ban on public housing for anyone convicted of a drug crime or other "safety-threatening" behavior. Parolees whose families reside in public housing—disproportionately African American and Latinx, again—suddenly had no place to go upon their release. Should they choose to stay with family anyway because they are required to be housed by the conditions of parole, they could immediately be sent back to prison, and the family members themselves can be kicked out of public housing for having taken in a relative with a felony record. Although technically public housing is governed by strict federal rules about housing discrimination according to race, the over-policing and over-incarceration of men and women of color ensure that the result is the same, as felony status becomes a stand-in for race. Meanwhile, the lack of housing and employment resulting from these conditions, again, ensure that the cycle of recidivism and incarceration will continue.

Perhaps nothing is more starkly indicative of the impact of race and incarceration on the fabric of the nation than the existence of felon disenfranchisement laws. Every state, with the exception of Vermont and Maine, has enacted some form of voter disenfranchisement for people with criminal convictions. These range from only disenfranchising people who are currently in prison (14 states and the District of Columbia[11]), to permanently banning those with a

---

[11] These are Hawaii, Illinois, Indiana, Massachusetts, Maryland, Michigan, Montana, New Hampshire, North Dakota, Ohio, Oregon, Pennsylvania, Rhode Island, and Utah.

felony conviction from voting in their lifetime, whether in or out of prison (12 states[12]). These laws have roots in both English law, which called for the "civil death" of those convicted of certain felonies, and in the Civil War, after which many states rushed to pass these laws to blunt the voting power of newly freed and enfranchised Black slaves. The effects have been severe: today, 6.1 million Americans are banned from voting due to a felony conviction, and one in every thirteen African Americans is banned from voting (compared to one in every fifty-six non-Black voters). In three states (Florida, Kentucky, and Virginia), more than one in every five African American adults is banned for life from voting. The impact of these laws on the electorate cannot be overstated: in essence, the nation has re-created the effects of slavery by disproportionately removing African Americans from the voting rosters, thereby politically re-entrenching the disempowerment of already marginalized minorities and altering the course of American history with the consequent shrunken and white-washed electorate.[13]

The conclusion is inescapable that the mantra of "colorblindness," which was solidified during the Obama presidency, obscures and exacerbates the distinctly and obviously racialized features of incarceration, reentry, and the communities affected most by them. In prisons, colorblindness is not even attempted, it is such a defining feature of the institution and its daily operations. While this can be blunted through work and self-help programs, education, sports and religious practice that integrate the incarcerated population, it is never absent. Upon reentry after release, the social, economic, and political realities of race and class-based stratification again confront this already marginalized population, with severe and far-reaching

---

12 These are Alabama, Arizona, Delaware, Florida, Iowa, Kentucky, Mississippi, Nebraska, Nevada, Tennessee, Virginia, and Wyoming.

13 In at least two recent presidential elections—those resulting in the presidencies of Donald Trump and George W. Bush—the disenfranchisement of Black voters in Florida and elsewhere literally tipped the scales. Had these individuals been able to vote, polls and estimates suggest that Al Gore and Hillary Clinton would have instead been elected.

consequences for the individuals, their families and communities, and our entire socio-political structure. Therefore, it is imperative that the lessons learned through the commonality of purpose in education, rehabilitation, and religion be translated into the non-incarcerated community with distinct care and an eye toward exposing and avoiding the pitfalls of "colorblindness."

Reconstructing the Moral Claim of Racially Unjust Mass Incarceration

Alison Benders[1]

The participants of this Roundtable and the essays in this volume have explored the criminalization of black and brown bodies from a diverse array of positions: formerly incarcerated people; employees of social service-reintegration organizations; prison ministers; social ethicists; lawyers and legal justice advocates; and sociologists. My contribution from theological anthropology can seem sterile and distant because theoretical foundations seem to lack pragmatic impact. Theological anthropology explores who we are as human beings in light of our faith commitments, who we are before God and who we are to each other. However, in and through prophetic exploration, theology can objectify our underlying conceptual framework for critique and reformulation. More adequate concepts can yield more effective exchanges in our day-to-day lives. So this essay attempts to

---

[1] Alison M. Benders, J.D., Ph.D., serves as Associate Dean and Senior Lecturer at the Jesuit School of Theology of Santa Clara University. In addition to administrative responsibilities, she teaches theological anthropology, emphasizing an intersectional exploration of human beings as enmeshed in society and culture. Her research focuses on questions of racial privilege and oppression. Her prayer book, *Just Prayer: A Liturgy of Hours for Peacemakers and Justice Seekers,* received the 2016 Catholic Publishing Best Book Award for Spirituality.

demonstrate that a better theological anthropology can disclose the social sin of mass incarceration and elevate its moral claim upon all of us in American society.

My experimental contribution begins by situating the theological discussion within the evidence that mass incarceration criminalizes people of color. This criminalization rests on an 'arm-chair' theology that valorizes human autonomy and equates disobedience with sinfulness. The second section presents an alternate theology of human identity based upon our social context of shared community and intersubjectivity. The next section shows what can happen when our understanding of the human person shifts *from* autonomous individualism epitomized in freedom *to* human community in which we are loved and we love others into full human flourishing. It focuses particularly on our obligation to address social sins because we are socially constituted. The concluding point is that, by understanding our humanity socially, our moral integrity compels us to claim social injustices as our own responsibility and address them.[2]

The Criminalization of People Because of Skin Color

Since the 1980's our nation has seen the skyrocketing rate of incarceration nearly quadrupling in 35 years to 7 million people under supervision by corrections departments, and more than 2.2 million in jails.[3] The Sentencing Project's 2013 report to the United

---

[2] The reflection here is particularly relevant to expanding efforts to repent for and redeem American culture from its 'original sin' of racism. I recognize that this topic far exceeds the limits of the Lane Center Roundtable Discussion and the present volume of collected essays; it is a tiny contribution that might respond to Black Catholic theologians' call for Christian theology to make anti-black racism a compelling theological issue.

[3] "Report of The Sentencing Project to the United Nations Human Rights Committee Regarding Racial Disparities in the United States Criminal Justice System," (2013) accessed August 31, 2017, published in full at The Sentencing Project, www.sentencingproject.org, 1.

Nations Human Rights Commission documents the racial disparity in the US criminal justice system. A few statistics, quoted directly from the report, provide ample evidence:

- "Roughly 12% of the United States population is black. Yet in 2011, black Americans constituted 30% of persons arrested for a property offense and 38% of persons arrested for a violent offense." (3)
- "Between 1980 and 2000, the U.S. black drug arrest rate rose from 6.5 to 29.1 per 1,000 persons; during the same period, the white drug arrest rate increased from 3.5 to 4.6 per 1,000 persons." (4)
- "[T]he Bureau of Justice Statistics found ... black drivers were twice as likely to experience the use or threat of violent force at the hands of police officers than both white and Hispanic drivers." (5)

The report concludes, based upon deeper statistical analysis, that implicit racial bias at every level of the criminal justice system is the predominant cause for the hyper-enforcement of criminal laws against men and women of color.

More problematically, utilizing the criminal justice system to control men and women of color represents the contemporary manifestation and state-sanctioned reinvention of slavery, Jim Crow segregation, northern ghettoization and unrelenting race-based violence. It expresses America's white supremacist culture built *ab initio* upon the dehumanization, exclusion and criminalization of non-white people.[4] The trajectory from slavery to today's prison system leads Loïc Wacquant to judge:

---

[4] Loïc Wacquant, "From Slavery to Mass Incarceration: Rethinking the 'Race Question' in the US." *New Left Review* 13, (2002): 55-56. See also Michelle Alexander, *The New Jim Crow: Mass Incarceration in the Age of Color Blindness* (New York: New Press, 2011).

> The astronomical overrepresentation of blacks in houses of penal confinement and the increasingly tight meshing of the hyperghetto with the carceral system suggests that, owing to America's adoption of mass incarceration as a queer social policy designed to discipline the poor and contain the dishonored, lower-class African-Americans now dwell, not in a society with prisons as their white compatriots do, but in the first genuine prison society in history.[5]

There are many approaches to address the racial discrimination in the criminal justice system. Some seek to reform the system directly by challenging facially neutral laws with disparate impact.[6] Bryan Stevenson's personal account in *Just Mercy: A Story of Justice and Redemption*[7] and Michelle Alexander's magisterial study, *The New Jim Crow*, are two instances of the vast scholarly and personal literature about the implicit bias and other injustices in the system itself. Moving from direct witness against racial injustice, a second approach seeks to reform the impact of the penal system more comprehensively by replacing its crippling adherence to retributive justice with a restorative justice model. Restorative justice augments a rights-punishment analysis with a focus on the dignity of the victims and offenders and on their community context in order to promote long-term social stability and even reconciliation.[8] All remedial efforts rest upon irrefutable evidence that our so-called justice system incarcerates people of color, especially black men, because of their skin color: it is a crime in our nation to have black or brown skin.

---

[5] Wacquant, 60.

[6] On the discriminatory impact of facially neutral policies and practices, see Eduardo Bonilla-Silva, *Racism without racists: Color-blind racism and the persistence of racial inequality in the United States* (Maryland: Rowman & Littlefield Publishing, 2010).

[7] Spiegel & Grau, 2015.

[8] Two examples are William O'Neill, "Imagining Otherwise: The Ethics of Social Reconciliation," *Journal of the Society of Christian Ethics* 22, (2002): 183–199; and Howard Zehr, *The Little Book of Restorative Justice: Revised and Updated* (New York: Good Books, 2014).

Reframing Our Understanding of the Human Person

Our common-sense concepts of sin and crime derive almost as an intellectual reflex from an ill-informed theological position. An untutored reading of Genesis can glean from the story of 'the Fall' that human beings are first and foremost free and autonomous individuals[9] who have disobeyed the only command God gives them. Sin is personal, intentional disobedience or transgression that offends God and/or other people.[10] An atonement theology, following upon the premise of freedom, reduces to God creates human beings to be free and obedient to God's will; human beings sin by disobeying God; human beings should bear the consequences of their sin; and, if not for Christ's sacrificial death, human beings would suffer death

---

[9] There is a much larger discussion here about whether freedom is a theoretical presumption for human identity or a primal experience. Regardless, the call by many contemporary theologians of color to root human identity in concrete and particularized experience represents a vital imperative. See, e.g., M. Shawn Copeland, *Enfleshing Freedom: Body, Race, and Being* (Minneapolis, MN: Fortress Press, 2010); Ada María Isasi-Díaz, *En la Lucha (In the Struggle): A Hispanic Women's Liberation Theology* (Augsburg Fortress Publishing, 1993); and James H. Cone, *A Black Theology of Liberation* (New York: Orbis Books, 1970). To revision the starting point of theological anthropology does not deny the experience of freedom to be an inextricable aspect of humanity; it merely recognizes that the meaning and expression of freedom cannot be abstracted from its cultural context.

[10] See Kenneth R. Himes, "Social Sin and the Role of the Individual," *The Annual of the Society of Christian Ethics* 6, (1986): 183-218, at 183 quoting Langdon Gilkey, "The language about Adam and Eve in the garden has represented the language of freedom, choice, act and responsibility; the language about our common inheritance [original sin] has represented that of necessity, fate, and so of universality and inevitability," from *Message and Existence: An Introduction to Christian Theology*, (Wipf and Stock Publishers, 2001): 112. Thus, 'sin' can refer to individual transgression or the given (and distorted) conditions in our human world. See also Bryan N. Massingale, *Racial justice and the Catholic Church* (New York: Orbis Books, 2014), 91-96; and Neil Ormerod, *Grace and Disgrace: A Theology of Self-Esteem, Society and History* (E.J. Dwyer, 1992), generally Part B.

as a consequence of sin. In this reductionist model, conformity with God's law constitutes the measure of human worthiness, love and ultimately, salvation. Its logic affirms for both sinners and criminals: those who break the law should be punished; those who are punished must have broken the law. Without a more adequate investigation into human identity, this legalistic theological anthropology leads us to accept, rather than abhor, the hyper-incarceration of people of color. Incarceration statistics then reinforce our cultural bias, particularly that dark skin equates with criminality.

—*Human beings as intersubjectively and socially constituted*

The problem with reducing human identity to freedom, and the resulting emphasis on punishment, is that it rests on a foundational notion of human identity that prescinds from our lived experience. An alternate starting point is to recognize that our humanity is in fact forged intersubjectively—in relationship. [11] We are rooted by our very existence in social relationships and mutual care. As co-creators with God, humanity's highest calling is to love other people into full human flourishing, just as God's love creates and sustains us. We ourselves are loved into our humanity by our parents, teachers, friends and most intimate partners. When we begin our theological anthropology here, interpersonal justice is the virtue that "perfects our relationships with other people," according to social ethicist James Keenan, SJ.[12] Thus, freedom is subsumed and contextualized within interpersonal and community relationships.

Catholic social teaching glosses the embodiment of justice by highlighting a moral obligation to solidarity. As Pope John Paul II explains: "[Solidarity] is not a feeling of vague compassion or shallow

---

[11] For a recent collection of diverse approaches to theological anthropology, see Lieven Boeve, Yves De Maeseneer, and Ellen Van Stichel, eds, *Questioning the Human: Toward a Theological Anthropology for the Twenty-First Century* (Oxford University Press, 2014).

[12] Lisa Fullam and Gina Hens-Piazza, unpublished paper, citing James Keenan, SJ, "Proposing Cardinal Virtues," *Theological Studies* 56, no.4 (2004): 709-729, 724.

distress at the misfortunes of so many people, both near and far. On the contrary, it is a firm and persevering determination to commit oneself to the common good; that is to say, to the good of all and of each individual, because we are all really responsible for all."[13] M. Shawn Copeland writes: "Solidarity is a task, a praxis through which responsible relationships between and among persons (between and among groups) may be created and expressed, mended and renewed. ... [T[he fundamental obligations that arise in the context of these relationships stem not from identity politics or from the erasure of difference, but rather from basic human creatureliness and love."[14]

With this reframing, the primary indicator of authentic humanity is the quality of our love as lived in relationship with others.[15] Human freedom is no longer untethered and privatized, but is located within a social nexus and the overarching obligations of solidarity and common good. This reframing still allows for a culturally contextualized investigation of freedom and responsibility, but it must be anchored in a particular community's history, traditions and values. When personal freedom and responsibility are abused, we investigate not just individual choices, but more importantly, how our communities practice interpersonal justice and embody mutual care, solidarity and justice for all members.

—*An intersubjective anthropology reveals social sin*

An intersubjective theological anthropology also clarifies what social sin is and our responsibility for it. Preoccupied with individual freedom and culpability, the criminal justice system only rarely asks about compulsion or 'bondage of the will,' mostly in particular situations of

---

[13] John Paul, I. I. "Encyclical Letter Sollicitudo Rei Socialis." *Vatican City: Libreria Editrice Vaticana* (1987), 38.

[14] M. Shawn Copeland, "The New Anthropological Subject at the Heart of the Mystical Body of Christ," *Proceedings of the Catholic Theological Society of America* 53, (2013): 37.

[15] Rooting human identity in intersubjectivity evokes notions of Trinity and the loving relationship among Father, Son and Spirit. Such a theological analysis is far beyond the scope of this discussion.

mental illness or abuse. With a similar focus, sin 'properly so called' is individual sin. Social sin has been understood as sin only analogously, because people cannot be blamed for harm for unintentional acts.[16] Individual sin looks backward in time toward a past injury to assign culpability and impose penance for disobedience to God's law. An individual focus precludes inquiry into the facticity of our social environment and the way the conditions of the world (i.e., original sin) truly constrain our freedom to act justly and lovingly. This approach to sin has tended to overpunish individuals for transgressions and overexculpate individuals for sinful systems and structures, precisely as displayed in the racial injustice of mass incarceration.

Human intersubjectivity and solidarity in community disclose our responsibility for the sin embedded in our institutions; they reveal to us our responsibility to create and sustain the common good and goodness in community. Exploring the implications of social sin, moral theologian Kenneth Himes parses responsibility for social sin according to three categories: causal, culpable and remedial.[17] *Causal responsibility* identifies the agents whose actions produce the physical or psychological harm. Causal responsibility may or may not be blameworthy, as in accidents where inattention causes harm. *Culpability* designates the agents who are to blame for the harm. The theological tradition distinguishes a personally and morally culpable act (a sin) based on intent to cause harm; moral condemnation for a "personally wrongful act" attaches only to intended injuries.[18] *Liability*, or remedial responsibility, specifies which agents are obliged to ameliorate a harm; liability might be direct for one's own actions

---

[16] See, e.g., Mark O'Keefe, *What are They Saying about Social Sin?* (Paulist Press, 1990); and Kristin E. Heyer, "Social sin and immigration: good fences make bad neighbors." *Theological Studies* 71, no. 2 (2010): 410-436, 415-420. See also Himes at 196-97, who does not rule out the possibility of assigning individual blame for collective action to group members, but cautions that this requires a careful analysis of causal contribution, voluntariness, one's role within the group and the actual practices and policies of the group.

[17] Himes, 189-91.

[18] Himes, 187.

or vicarious for another's acts due to legal or cultural conventions. These distinctions of responsibility allow a more effective analysis of the complex dialectic between individual and social responsibility, particularly with respect to liability for social sins.

In moving from blame to liability, Himes asks: "[W]hy should a person not be expected to do something to oppose a perceived [or proven] injustice?"[19] He suggests that the liability to remediate a cultural injustice attaches to everyone in the culture, and particularly to those who benefit most or who "unconsciously encourage [social sins] through a variety of folkways and social institutions."[20] He concludes: "[T]hose who have benefitted from the past structures should strive to assist those who have been disadvantaged by the culture. No judgment of blameworthiness is needed, only an assessment that the present cultural institutions … are institutions which [we] have more or less supported."[21] Regardless of whether we caused an injustice in the first place, we are *liable* for ameliorating social or institutionalized harms and reconstituting the interpersonal justice and common good that are the theological foundations of human community.

A More Compelling Moral Claim

The theological and experiential understanding of the human person as intersubjectively constituted in and through our relationships to others has tremendous power. So, what can happen when our theological understanding of the human person shifts *from* autonomous individualism epitomized in freedom *to* human community in which we are loved and we love others into full human flourishing? Most significantly, a foundational commitment to intersubjectivity

---

[19] Himes, 205. We need not turn the page on the past policies and actions that led to the mass incarceration or abandon reintegration and reconciliation measures. As noted in the introduction to this essay, these are vital and complementary aspects of a comprehensive battle against mass incarceration on individual, systemic, political and cultural and religious levels.
[20] Himes, 211.
[21] Himes, 212.

and solidarity highlights, through incongruity, the immorality of our society. It shows the hypocrisy of our professed commitment to interpersonal and social justice when one group of people is disproportionately oppressed and imprisoned. Rather than interrogate an offender, 'What did you do wrong?' we must ask, 'What are we doing wrong that this group of people is perpetually criminalized?' Rather than demand of those incarcerated, 'How will you atone for this?' society must consider, 'How will we assure the restoration of these people to full inclusion in our shared future?' These questions compel us to reexamine the underlying social inequities that drive so-called criminal behavior, and to search for something other than retribution and punishment as preferred methods of social control.

Particularly in the present discussion, beginning with intersubjectivity strengthens the moral claim that mass incarceration makes upon us because we are complicit in the injustice.[22] Regardless of the culpability of individual offenders, statistical evidence and human suffering testify that hyper-incarceration is a tool to criminalize people of color in their very existence. In the context of mass incarceration, social sin reveals itself precisely in documented patterns of injustice and discrimination. Thus, simply by being members of American society, we must act. If not, we are guilty of a sin of omission, either because we avoid recognizing what is common knowledge in the public sphere (vincible ignorance); or, we absolve ourselves with the usual justifications of indifference: "my efforts are too small to make a difference"; "others are taking care of this"; "I can't think of what to do;" or "it's not my area."[23] A just response requires, at the very least, support for efforts to reform the system, to reintegrate those

---

[22] Alexander Mikulich, Laurie Cassidy, and Margaret Pfeil, *The Scandal of White Complicity in US Hyper-incarceration: A Nonviolent Spirituality of White Resistance* (Springer, 2013).

[23] David Ford analyzes three levels of indifference relating to the sin of omission: awareness, acknowledgement and action. *Sins of omission: a primer on moral indifference* (Fortress Press, 1990). I have grouped awareness and acknowledgement together as vincible ignorance.

who have served their time and to eliminate the underlying inequities that created the problem.

Granted, this is a tall order. Still, only by acknowledging that our criminal justice system is unjust—by acknowledging that our nation excludes and criminalizes people for the color of their skin—can we take seriously the moral obligation rooted in our identity as co-creators of human community with God. Taking responsibility to mitigate the racial injustice in the prison system means intentionally cultivating new skills to become more personally active in restoring justice according to our means and opportunities. These demands must be particularized according to our individual situations, skills and capacities, but they cannot be ignored.

***

Theology is not an abstract drill. Rather it is a lever for personal and social change when we integrate our faith commitment into concrete action. A first step, offered here for all people whatever our situation, is a renewed theology, a better understanding of how we define ourselves as human beings. If we are to root out racial injustice, especially our own indifference, we must view human community intersubjectively—this means, in common parlance, that we must practice love. To love and to create the common good for our community means looking at the world through a lens of solidarity. Christ tells us to love one another as he has loved us. As people created in the image of God and imitating Christ's own abounding love, we must respond to the moral claim that sinful social structures make upon us as individuals, as a Church and as a nation. In short, a theological anthropology grounded in intersubjectivity and solidarity in community reveals the sinfulness of hyper-incarceration of people of color—and we must respond.

Beyond the Hidden University, Dana P. Harper II, ball point pen, 8.5x11 inches, California State Prison Solano, 2014

Envisioning Social Justice: From Theory to Practice

REGGIE DANIELS

Introduction

In this paper, I talk about social justice as it relates to my personal struggle with the criminal justice system—but also how my personal struggle led to community organizing through community-based organizations (CBO's). Community organizing led to navigating through systemic oppression and structural barriers at an organizational level. When I was a young person, I didn't have a voice, and there wasn't a fair system. I decided to choose education and research as a way of mapping a system that I had navigated that wasn't necessarily designed to hold me or to hold my success. Through education, I found a voice and a fair system. What "fair system" means to me is that there is a specific, explicit way to challenging unfair outcomes, unlike challenging discrimination, which is full of dark secrets and trapdoors and staircases that lead to nowhere.

The purpose of this paper is to share with readers how I met personal and organizational challenges by applying critical race theory. My research has provided windows into complex systems that were obscure to me and difficult to understand. Theory is like a handle on a hot pot on the stove, so that you can safely manage it. I seek healing for myself, and I seek to provide learning communities where healing can be fostered.

Personal Story

I started out as a young person with passions and dreams: a high school graduate, hoping to go to college. I was assaulted by three grown men, and I was the victim of a violent shooting. I was not supported by the criminal justice system; I was told that I "got what I deserved." My dream was deferred. At that time, someone from street life reached out to me, gave me a gun, gave me support in a place of trauma. Like so many people in the life, he meant well; he was reaching out to me in an authentic kind of way. But he was also duplicitous: he was a businessman, and he was recruiting workers.

I didn't know this until later, but because of the trauma I experienced, and the experience of violence, I decided that what they were doing was more powerful than what I was doing. I think that was the first time I thought: I was a black man trying to live in a white man's world. I felt like I had it all wrong, and I was vulnerable. So I put off trying to assimilate to white America, and put on a new lifestyle: the street lifestyle. That became more real, more relevant to me in terms of survival. What started out as a feeling of a deeper sense of blackness—of understanding my community better—someone turned into cycles of addiction, cycles of violence.

I would live in that world for the next decade and a half. I would be living in the drug life; weapons would be a part of my reality. I would promote myself as a drug dealer—not that I was ruthless. It was more preventative: *I'm not going to be the victim no more.* I built this armor up, because the weak get preyed upon. So I wanted to make sure that everything I displayed, everything I symbolized, was strong: king-of-the-jungle-strong, lion-strong.

In one way, I was safe—but in another way, I became vulnerable to the larger system of criminal justice. The fascination with the lifestyle, the drugs, and the material gain made me oblivious to the way that

I was set up to be victimized by the system, not by individual people anymore. I became a primary candidate for a system that Michelle Alexander describes as "the New Jim Crow"—a system that is based on forced labor.

I didn't realize the impact that this was having on my life until I started to feel the absolute absence of passion—the kind of passion that comes from knowing your purpose, from making real contributions of wisdom, truth, and justice. This was a moment of clarity for me in the midst of the allure of the power of the streets. I had become a major consumer of—and a product of—my own predatory survival skills. I had become a capitalist: I no longer valued community and relationships—people I loved, people I was close to, people I looked up to—but I only valued profit.

That went on for a decade and a half. It wasn't until I was incarcerated, and I turned 40 while I was inside. And I had a transformational experience: I was in one part of the jail, my son was in another part of the jail, and I was 40 years old. I felt the shameful experience all through my body: I cried, I lamented, and I made a decision to change and to never go back. I had decided to change before, but I had never closed the door or burned the bridge or said, *there is only forward.*

Then I felt the immediate need for a plan of action, because of the finality of that compelling force. Two mentors came to me and I said, *I'm ready.* I'm ready for programs, I'm ready for treatment, I'm ready to come out of denial. The way that I was holding those who were dependent on me for resources was actually the way that I had caged myself. I had never seen myself as trapped before, only as the trapper.

Experience With Organizations

The San Bruno County Jail is a "program facility," which means that its mission is not just to house inmates but also to have them involved in programs or in schooling, so that when they get out, they can face the challenges that led them to incarceration. The jail offers substance abuse programs, violence prevention programs, and the first in-custody charter high school. The programs that I participated in were the Roads to Recovery Substance Abuse Recovery Program, and the Resolve to Stop the Violence Project (RSVP), which is a violence prevention and intervention program. Community Works, a nonprofit organization, offers RSVP at the San Bruno County Jail through the San Francisco Sheriff's Department. ManAlive is the curriculum for RSVP; it is designed to restore the perpetrator's identity, and provide language and tools for participants to get their needs met in nonviolent ways. In these programs, I started my journey as a participant seeking to restore myself from the harms that I had endured; today, as a service provider, my process and journey within to restore myself continues.

When I began these programs, I started to share my experience and to journal. And then core issues emerged that I hadn't dealt with: my parents were addicts, so there was abandonment, and my parents died a month apart, so there was grief. These programs offered mentoring and therapeutic sessions; this personal work of journaling and dealing with my grief in a group setting gained me acknowledgement among staff and administrators, and I was selected for an internship. That internship led to my being a facilitator, and it made the Sheriff's Department interested in how my story might help others. ManAlive helped me to identify the fear and powerlessness that was behind the rage. I had been out there dying, when I really thought I had it all together.

Initially, my experience was about being the poster child for personal transformation: accolades, preferred treatment, opportunities. At first, that was really exciting, and it filled a deep-seated need for recognition that I had been getting from the drug life. Now that recognition was coming from working on myself and helping others, instead of material things and violence.

As I became more sophisticated, I also became more critical and analytical. Innovative ideas started to occur to me: in working on patterns in my own life, I started to see patterns in programs. Programs like mine had been around for 20 years, and yet recidivism remained at 70% or higher. It started to occur to me that this was a contradiction like the ones I had in my personal life around addiction—contradictions I had to face in order to grow. So I started to bring my ideas and innovations to the directors, who were in charge of the resources, hoping that they would be well-received. For example, the men in the group were being asked to journal their earliest experiences with violence—how they lost their innocence of violence, and how that escalated into incarceration. And what I noticed is that their personal stories were being kept in files, used by staff only when that participant acted out. So I started to ask the participants to bring their stories into the community, and to share them as a community-building exercise. The men in the group became excited; my group was already full, but there were more and more people who heard about this and wanted to get in. At this point, my thinking was that this would be supported and appreciated by my organization, but it actually resulted into my being called into a meeting and interrogated. At first, I had the sense that my ideas were being welcomed, but soon they began to be interpreted as critiques, not just ideas. And soon thereafter I became suspect.

A suspect is someone who might bring harm to the organization. Someone who is an ingrate, who is not grateful enough for opportunities. To me, I was simply pointing out opportunities for growth, which had been such a key component of my life. When I didn't feel heard, and I was being looked at as suspect, the passion for change didn't go away, but I decided that I needed a new strategy. And that led me to reconsider education in a new light. Coming out of high school, I saw education as a means to living a wealthy life. Now I see education as a means of liberation, for me and my community. In completing my doctorate, I am not merely concerned with earning higher wages. My greater concern is how the informational tools I've learned can be used to interrupt systems of oppression.

One of the first things I started to notice about these organizations is that the people who were being served could talk about their experiences, but they didn't have a voice in how their experiences were being shaped and defined. Their experiences were being told and shaped by people from other communities who didn't live close to the problems they were experiencing. For example, most of the participants in the program are African American; however, I'm the only African American facilitator, and the executive leadership is all white. Once again, it occurred to me that the vehicle that had once held me and seemed to protect me could also be a force that was oppressing me and holding me back—now it wasn't the drug gang, but it was an organizational level.

Theorizing the Journey

This newfound discovery of how oppression works is what drew me to critical race theory and authors like Tara J. Yosso, who theorize about community and cultural wealth in targeted and marginalized communities. Yosso speaks specifically about how community wisdom gets dismissed through academia, particularly deficit thinking—scholarship that blames the victims, claiming that they are lacking and denying their experience. This was extremely validating for me—to find the language for the experiences of people of color being damaged. Yosso's article, "Towards a Critical Theory of Whiteness," talks about how community-based organizations can have hierarchies, in which those who have white privilege shape policies and allocate resources, while people of color do the labor. It was at that moment that I realized I need to combine academics and scholarship with my experience coming from a marginalized, targeted group. To not come from deficit thinking—specifically, to not think that folks who are incarcerated are wicked or lacking, but are people whose dreams have been deferred and who have lost their way—was to claim my power. For me, Yosso illuminated how devaluing community cultural wealth creates bias and discrimination toward communities of color.

In particular, Yosso talks about community cultural wealth in two components: *navigational capital* and *resistance capital*. Navigational capital is when communities of color are able to safely matriculate institutions that are traditionally white or white-dominated, like the office of the presidency. Resistance capital is when communities of color are able to successfully circumvent oppressive forces from the dominant culture—for example, the Civil Rights Movement of the 60s. Reading Yosso's article helped me to see how the ManAlive curriculum—which was designed by an older white man—was being superimposed on the group. His curriculum took center stage in the class: the men's experiences of how they survived these communities where violence proliferated, and how their families had overcome years of systemic oppression, were just ignored. The participants were just asked to learn this curriculum as "beginners," and not as people who had valuable, useful information and experience. When the men tried to describe how their victimization from systemic oppression led to their violations, it was being interpreted through the program as collusion, denial, or a refusal to be accountable. In groups where I encourage these men to share their stories, I saw that in their stories were funds of knowledge: how they were able to safely navigate violence in communities where their survival, statistically, was very unlikely. Their personal stories actually gave *content* to the curriculum. So how can community cultural wealth be leveraged to mitigate deficit thinking and create healthy learning environments for programs like ManAlive?

In critical race theory, "interest convergence" is when the power structure will pass a law that appears to be in the interest of the subordinate or targeted group, but in the long-term, it serves to further oppressive forces. For example, *Brown vs. Board of Education* was supposed to desegregate schools: it did allow blacks to attend schools, but it actually ended up creating split school systems that furthered the marginalization of black communities, rather than closing the gap. In a similar way, the founder of RSVP believed that perpetrators of violence experience an identity crisis: they vacate their authentic selves to occupy a violent image. The claim is that the ManAlive curriculum will re-unify the person and their authentic self. But from my observations, too often participants become 'language brokers'— they learn the language of the curriculum, and use that language to mask the same behavior. I suspect that the absence of personal story and navigational capital robs the participants of that opportunity to deepen.

Scholars have argued that *culturally sustaining pedagogy* is essential in a culturally diverse, equitable society, and that education that fails to account for learners' cultural and linguistic backgrounds, contributes to the school-to-prison pipeline.[1,2] However, to my knowledge, little has been said about culturally sustaining pedagogy within the criminal justice system. My research seeks to use the community cultural capital in the room as evidence that communities of color have valuable capital—capital that is not acknowledged in spaces that rely on deficit theories to analyze and interpret the needs of people of color. How can community cultural capital be leveraged to increase client interest and lower recidivism rates? As Yosso states, "transgressive knowledges…can value the voices of People of Color, and can envision the margins as places empowered by transformative resistance."[3]

Applying these theories, I am now collaborating with Professor Amie Dowling on a project called The KNOWLEDGE SESSIONS, a gathering of educators, community members, and service providers who create a participant-focused learning community around experiences of incarceration—like a safe-house for people who are committed to continuing their process of development after incarceration. The KNOWLEDGE SESSIONS conducts practical, authentic, tangible, community-based research to further the work in social justice begun by the USF Performing Arts Department's Performing Arts and Community Exchange course (PACE) and RSVP. One of its unique qualities is that there is no curriculum;

---

[1] Gloria Ladson-Billings. "Toward a Theory of Culturally Relevant Pedagogy." *American Educational Research Journal* 32, no. 3 (1995): 465-91.

[2] Django Paris: "A friend who understand fully: Notes on Humanizing Research in a Multiethnic Youth Community." *International Journal of Qualitative Studies in Education* 24, no. 2 (2011): 137-149.

[3] Tara J. Yosso. "Whose culture has capital? A critical race theory discussion of community cultural wealth." *Race, Ethnicity and Education* 8, no.1 (2005): 69-91.

the curriculum will be developed by the participants' interaction and by the needs they define for themselves. The group is in its early developmental phase, but it is our effort to build organic learning communities and disrupt the harms created by systemic oppression.

By establishing a safe learning community, we make a space for men and women of color, in particular, to walk onto a campus that they have been conditioned to believe is not open to them—and to undertake their own meaningful research projects there. In this space, we are using creative forms of expression to challenge oppression, create and sustain relationships; we are merging social activism, facilitation skills, and artistic practices in theater, dance and music as tools for social change. In accordance with USF's vision and the model of the PACE class, the KNOWLEDGE SESSIONS is structured as community-based research: this is not something being done *for*, but rather something being done *with*—we are collaborating, everyone serves and everyone is served.

What I see, looking back now, is that there are two journeys: a personal journey from thinking I had the answer, to disappointment, hurt, and loss; and a journey in organizations, from thinking I had the answer to bias and discrimination. But I finally found something that has intrinsic value: the power to learn and the power to teach. That has never failed me.

Art Between the Bars:
In Search of Self and Fellowship

LARRY BREWSTER[1] AND CUONG TRAN[2]

Arts in Corrections: A Brief Introduction

What follows this brief introduction to the Arts in Corrections Program is a narrative that features the voices of individuals who discovered through artistic expression a way to transform their identities from "correctional numbers" to "artists" and human Beings.

> *California involvement with prison arts began in the 1970s; Jerry Brown was serving his first term as Governor and artist Eloise Smith was executive director of the California Arts Council (CAC). Governor Brown asked Eloise to investigate the arts in social institutions, including prisons.*

---

[1] Dr. Larry Brewster is Professor Emeritus and former dean at the University of San Francisco. Before joining USF, he was academic dean at Menlo College, and prior to that, Dean of the School of Liberal Studies and Public Affairs at Golden Gate University, and professor and associate dean at San Jose State University. He regularly consults in public policy and program evaluation, and is author of journal articles and books, including The Public Agenda: Issues in American Politics, 5th edition, Wadsworth & Company, 2004; A Primer of California Politics, 2nd edition, Wadsworth & Company, 2004; and Paths of Discovery: Art Practice and Its Impact in California Prisons, 2nd edition, Createspace & Company, 2015.

[2] Cuong Tran is a gifted artist who finds through his art practice inner-peace, gratitude, and fellowship. He generously shares his talents, insights and time with other inmates, no matter their race, ethnicity or affiliations.

She concluded in her 1976 report that there was more art activity in the prison system than in any other state institution. Eloise was impressed by the enthusiasm and raw talent shown by many of the inmates—and by the impact that art practice appeared to have on the lives of the artists.

Soon after leaving the Arts Council, she and her husband, historian and writer Page Smith, designed a pilot program—the Prison Arts Project—and secured funding through grants. The Smiths conducted a fine arts program at Vacaville State Prison—chosen because the inmates had already formed their own unofficial art guild and had let Eloise know during one of her visits that as serious artists they hungered for formal instruction, supplies, and a place in which to work.

The pilot program at Vacaville was an enormous success, resulting in authorization by the state legislature of funding for a prison arts program modeled after the Prison Arts Project. The law was signed by Governor Brown in 1980, creating Arts in Corrections (AIC). Arts in Corrections provided inmates with instruction and mentoring in visual, literary, and performing arts as well as fine craft disciplines. Although Eloise did not intend for AIC to be a job training program leading to a career in the arts, she did believe that the artistic process could provide inmates with heightened opportunities for solving problems, developing self-discipline, exercising impulse control, and improving confidence and self-esteem—all important building blocks in preparing inmates for life after prison.

Her vision compelled Eloise to insist from the outset that the arts program employ only trained, active, and successful artist-instructors. She believed inmates would benefit from the professional artists' excitement about their own work, and would learn through them that the artistic process demands focused attention, hard work, and self-discipline.

My more than 30 years' association with AIC as the principle evaluator of the program confirms Eloise's vision and expected outcomes. I first conducted a cost-benefit study in 1983, and for the past ten years, I have been interviewing and surveying inmate-artists. returned citizen artists, and artist-instructors. My research, and that of others' in Europe, New Zealand, Australia, and other prison arts programs, shows a strong correlation between art practice and intellectual, social, and emotional growth. The following interview is just one of many examples of the positive impact of prison arts programming.

(Brewster/Merts, Paths of Discovery: Art Practice and Its Impact in California Prisons, 2nd ed.).

This is a story about incarcerated and returned citizen artists who, through their writing, drawing, painting, music, theater, or any number of other artistic, creative pursuits, often find their unknown self, and in turn, better understand and accept the person they were prior to incarceration. In the process, they find fellowship with other artists, regardless of race, ethnicity, gang affiliation, or crime—in what is an otherwise cold, dangerous and isolating environment.

I've had the pleasure—privilege, really—to spend time with hundreds of inmate artists over the past 10 years, including interviews with more than 50 currently and formerly incarcerated men and women (primarily men) who participated in Arts in Corrections, a fine arts program offered in each of the California state prisons, and celebrating its 40th anniversary this year. Those interviewed represented a broad range of people, measured by age, crime, length of time served, race, ethnicity, and temperament. Some were experienced artists at the time of their incarceration, while most had still to discover their innate creative talent. Nearly everyone learned the value of hard work, self-discipline, and the importance of completing projects. A common refrain was the value of having a safe place—the art rooms—where they could let their guard down, concentrate on their projects, and enjoy and trust fellow artists of every color. In those spaces they were artists, not simply numbers, and skin color wasn't an issue.

I choose to focus on an Asian-American inmate artist whose story I believe best captures the truth on how prison arts empowers men and women to do their time meaningfully—gaining self-confidence, patience, discipline, and knowing how it feels to complete projects successfully. A perfect example is when Cuong, a Vietnamese gifted artist-inmate, took an interest in Matt, a young African-American who grew up in a rough dysfunctional household. Matt is an active gang member who works in the prison library. Cuong took him under his wing, helping Matt to discover his hidden talents in drawing and painting. Cuong taught Matt to draw and eventually convinced him to open up about his life through self-help groups and his drawings.

Cuong found that Matt was much more than a "loud, seemingly dangerous gang member."

Matt told me he never cared much for art more than to say, "Wow! That is really cool" when looking at someone else's work. All his life he had focused on being the sole provider for his family, keeping them together and out of the system. He felt art, like so many other things, was a luxury and out of reach for him or his family. He then tells of his time in prison, when he found it difficult, if not impossible, to express himself other than through gang violence. To his astonishment, he discovered, with Cuong's help, his hidden talent for drawing, and expressing through his art "beautiful, yet controversial messages."

Matt spoke of his feelings that "prison is designed to dictate every aspect of your life, to cut you off from the world, and destroy any vestige of a life you had." It has been his experience that "prison staff are trained to control what you think, how you act, and who you talk to. Their goal is to conform you to a life of complacency by destroying your ambitions and dreams." Art for Matt, and for so many other men and women I've interviewed, is a unique and powerful tool for freedom, hope, and inspiration, and offers a path for achieving your full potential as a human being. Although Matt has finished only a few pieces in a relatively short time as a practicing artist, he feels good about his progress as an artist, and his growth as a person. As he put it, "every time I start a new project, I try something new. Art has helped me grow far more than I imagined possible, and in a relatively short time. I think it is because I now found a healthy avenue to express the hurt and pain that I feel, but also the hope and strength that I possess. I want to focus on resisting perceived wrongs, and truly make a difference in my corner of the world. I am grateful to Cuong, my fellow artist and teacher."

Cuong always dabbled in art as a child and adolescent. He vividly remembers his very first attempt to draw the little chipmunk characters, Chip and Dale, in a Disney book. He was 4 years old when he took a sheet of paper and a pencil and drew the picture as he saw it, happily showing his parents when done. They asked, "Did you trace it?" He was upset when they didn't believe that it was his own work. He remembers feeling defensive when he told them he did not trace it, pointing out that the picture he drew was much larger than the one in the book.

His parents made photocopies of that picture and the subsequent ones he drew. They showed their friends and family, and Cuong was thrilled that his talents were appreciated, and that his parents were proud of him. When his parents couldn't afford the latest and greatest toys, he set out to create his own with paper and cardboard. He knew in his heart that he was going to be an artist when he grew up.

It turned out his plans changed in middle school. His parents began to instill in him the importance of "becoming successful." They presented three career choices: doctor, engineer, or lawyer, with an emphasis on doctor. He remembers talking with them about his love of art, and his desire to make a living as an artist. Their response was simple and direct: "Son, artists don't make money." Cuong laughed as he told me, "That more or less ended the discussion." In high school, Cuong used every opportunity to use his artistic skills on class projects, but any dreams of "being an artist" were already diminished. As he got older, school and work took priority. Art wasn't just placed on the backburner—it was taken off the stove.

Fast forward some years and he found himself in prison, with a long sentence in a level 4 prison. In his words, "[he] had lots of time to sit with nothing to do." As a way of passing time, and to fight against depression, he began drawing again. He had a bit of a rusty start after so many years of not actively using the right side of his brain. Enrolling in Arts in Corrections provided him with the opportunity to regain "his brush strokes," learn new techniques, and engage the artist-teachers and fellow inmates. It wasn't long before his "drawing skills were on a par with the best of them."

Cuong sent his work home to his wife. It is sometimes said that an artist's work is a reflection of the soul, mind, and heart. He believed this to be true for him. At the beginning of his prison sentence, his work reflected what he missed most, his wife, and he drew a great number of portraits of her. As he looks back on those days, he found words were inadequate to express his love and pain and discovered art as his way of expressing a longing for her and their simple life before prison.

One of the most difficult conditions of prison life for Cuong is the racial segregation imposed on inmates by correctional policies and gang affiliations. The art classrooms are among the very few spaces that bridge the racial divide when working on his art or in class. Cuong, like so many other art students, felt he could "drop the mask" prisoners wear as a defense mechanism. One of the first artists Cuong got to know was a Puerto Rican named Jerry, who works in various art mediums. In time, Cuong considered him a brother. They loved sharing ideas and concepts as they explored their own and each other's work. They agreed that typical prison art can be stagnant, and how grateful they were for the gift of the artist-teachers who encourage and inspire them every day. They talk about how instrumental the teachers are in giving them the confidence to expand their vision and think outside of their own "box."

Cuong has interacted with some very talented and intelligent prisoners—artistic and otherwise—who are insecure, trapped by their limited experiences even prior to prison, and who are now at the lowest ebb of their self-esteem and confidence. He is reminded that a "fear of failure" causes problems for any of us, and especially prisoners. These experiential and emotional limitations are both expressed in their art, and frequently resolved through their art practice—with the help of their teachers and fellow artists.

Cuong has seen many beautiful pieces of art created behind bars. However, as Jerry and Cuong discussed, the themes and styles don't differ all that much. This is especially true for inmates of different racial and cultural heritage. He believes any artist with a trained eye can tell you if a drawing or painting was created by a "White, Brown, Black, or Yellow" inmate. Skulls usually are drawn by White inmates, "Aztec" style by Hispanics, dragons and koi fish by Asians, and brick walls and street signs by Blacks. Cuong, for example, was often asked to draw "Asian" style artwork by inmates and prison staff, but he didn't want to pigeon-hole himself by acquiescing.

He felt the prison culture was overdue for a shock. He also felt stagnated when drawing with graphite pencils. He decided it was time for him to experiment with 3-D sculptures. With the help of artist-teachers and the materials provided by the prison arts program, he forged ahead. His choice of subject wasn't the usual Harley-Davidson motorcycle or pinup girl, which is so familiar and frequent in prison. Instead, his first sculpture was a red demon with wings and glowing yellow eyes. While he had never before sculpted, he fell back on his mechanical background when constructing the skeletal frame. His first sculpture was crudely made, but he kept it as a reminder of his progression in this art medium.

He remembers fondly the response from other inmates and prison staff. They were blown away! As he continued to sculpt and create, the most common response was, "I have *never* seen anything like that created in prison." This was from inmates and prison staff alike, many of whom had been in the system for decades. Cuong was encouraged to continue making art by prison staff, inmates and free artists who taught in the program. It was then that Cuong knew that he had the power within him to spark change both in himself and in others. He wanted to show the world that there are decent, talented people in prison. Art allows him, and others, to show the world that he (they) are still human beings, that he (they) are not defined by his (their) worst decision. He (they) use their art practice as the means for eliminating, or at least modifying, the negative stereotypes of prisoners. He wasn't the only inmate-artist whose creativity and hard, disciplined work led to positive, life-affirming encouragement.

A few years ago, Cuong showed some of his work to his supervisor, the Senior Librarian, who was very impressed, to say the least. Cuong then suggested hosting an art contest in the library as a means of promoting healthy competition and improving self-esteem. He worked with his supervisor and the prison administration to define the parameters of the contest, including allowing the inmate population to cast a vote for their favorite piece of art. It has been a huge success, with each participant bringing their A-game. They are currently working on their fifth art contest.

The art program and subsequent contests helped to open communication between inmates of different classifications. Cuong has found that staff, artists, other inmates and free citizens are positively affected by art. The reactions to the "masterpieces" produced for the contests bring a sense of pride and accomplishment to the participating inmates; they now have tangible evidence that their hard work and creative spirit pays off. One of the most important lessons Cuong has learned is that art has the ability to transcend race, religion, creed, affiliation and orientation. It is through art that he has been able to meet and collaborate with people from every conceivable background—people with whom he normally would not have crossed paths, except as potential enemies. This is a theme I've heard over and over again in my interviews with inmate-artists, and that I have observed in the dozens of classrooms I've visited in the past ten years.

Art showings and contests are not unique to Cuong's prison. There have been similar events held most every year, and at each of the state prisons since the founding of Arts in Corrections 40 years ago. These events are great opportunities for each prison to put their best foot forward in their respective communities. Community leaders and citizens are invited to experience inmates in a context different than, say television shows such as "Lockdown." Witnessing inmates acting in plays, performing their music, hearing them read their poetry or prose, seeing their paintings and sculptures, and engaging them in Q & A sessions is mind-expanding, and it has been a profound experience for me. It is nearly impossible to leave these events without at least being open to accepting the possibility of rehabilitation, and accepting the artists as people who are more than their worst mistake.

Cuong told me of a university near his prison that invited inmates to display their work in the campus library, resulting in an ongoing collaboration between the prison and university. Cuong was invited to spearhead the project from his end. Inmates were invited to include biographies along with their artwork. At the conclusion of the first exhibit, they were able to read the comment book. The feedback from the community and students was amazing. Once again, the participating inmates were exposed to positive reinforcement through their art. As Cuong put it, "What a self-esteem boost!" He is confident that their art changed many perspectives about prison.

Cuong's wife and family were able to see the exhibit. His wife let him know just how much comfort she enjoys knowing that his time is being used constructively. The exhibit, she told him, provided her with proof of his rehabilitation. There are many things he doesn't share with his wife, such as the violence and injustice he witnesses and endures daily. He has said that "his crime hurt her and their relationship enough." However, his art plays a significant role in enabling her to support his work, and is keeping them united for a common cause, despite their physical separation.

Through the university exhibit, Cuong was able to reunite with his estranged father. He happened to be visiting in the United States at the time of the exhibit. Cuong's sister informed his father of the exhibit and he was adamant about seeing it in person. Coincidentally, Cuong had called his sister on a whim, not knowing his father was in the country. He spoke with his father for the first time in over nine years. His father told him how proud he was of him and all he had accomplished while in prison. This affirmation was out of the ordinary, since his father had rejected him when he was arrested, convicted and sentenced. They were able to arrange an in-person visit, at which time Cuong made amends to his father. They have remained in close touch ever since. Cuong repeated his new refrain, "Oh, the power of art!"

I have heard so many other inmate-artists speak about how they reconnected, or deepened, their family ties through their art. This is true for their children, wives, grandmothers, girlfriends, and fathers. Similar to Cuong, they have discovered for themselves the therapeutic value of art while on their prison journey. It allows them to be free despite being physically restricted. In an environment where their every move is monitored and controlled, their ideas, creativity, and imagination are the only things that are limitless. Art is freedom. It lets them put a part of themselves on paper, or in a sculpture, or through music, or theater. Art, in any of its forms, brings a voice to the forgotten, who are little more than a number.

Inmate-artists, including Cuong, are generally active in self-help groups and pursue other educational and vocational programs. Cuong's experience is similar to others in these programs, finding them of value, some more than others, but each with its merits. For example, the group or class size tends to be large and less personal than the typical art classes. Also, the curriculum is generalized and taught at you, not with you—you are the passive learner. The goal for each participant is to internalize the lessons, applying them to their individual lives. Yet, Cuong asks, "How can these lessons be quantified?" He notes that most often "there are not follow-up sessions to measure an individual's rehabilitative progress." This sounds a little like education everywhere.

Cuong truly believes that an art program provides greater opportunity for rehabilitation, and it is easier to gauge an inmate's progress. He understands that art isn't for everyone, and that inmates should take advantage of every course and group available to them. But for him, and for so many of his fellow artists, the art curriculum, mentorship provided by professional, practicing artist-teachers, and finished artwork, writing or music projects are essential to enhancing inmate self-esteem, confidence, and feelings of accomplishment.

Outside of the art classes, Cuong—along with many other Arts in Corrections artists—offers to assist inmates if they want to learn, for example, how to draw. He is especially proud of an approach to drawing which he developed and is sharing with fellow inmates of all heritages. This motivation was in part to demonstrate how art practice can help improve behavior, and it lends itself to gauging progress. He started an unofficial drawing class in the prison library. He created a simple curriculum where students can look at a drawing that has been broken down into smaller squares. This allows, according to Cuong, "students to view a possibly intimidating and monumental project as smaller, manageable pieces". He goes on to say that "there are a series of drawings that the students can complete at their leisure. The pictures get progressively more detailed as the students gain confidence in their abilities."

Cuong reports that nearly every student begins his classes with low self-esteem. As he offers this program to any inmate who inquires, he often hears them say, "I can't draw. I suck," or "I already know I can't draw." He finds that the hardest aspect for him is to convince the guy to "give it a shot." Once they risk taking the first class, most of them are hooked.

As his students complete the lessons, he has them submit their drawings for "evaluation." Even before he sees their work, most of the men are making excuses for why their drawings aren't "perfect." Cuong believes this is a measure of their low self-esteem and confidence. He always is very gentle in his review of their work. He doesn't want to discourage anyone, especially anyone trying to gain a new skill. Instead, as with any good teacher, he focuses on what they did well, rather than on their flaws. He emphasizes that art is more about individuality, and that "perfect" is in the eye of the beholder. He points out that most inmates are subjected to abuse and humiliation, not positive reinforcement. In his own way, and through art, he wants to combat a prisoner's dehumanizing and demeaning life behind bars.

Cuong has witnessed "hardcore criminals" blush and shyly smile like 5-year-old school boys as he gives them praise for their efforts. Many times, it takes *months* before the men trust him enough to take compliments. Slowly, they accept that he is genuine in his praise, and that the praise is not generalized but applies to each student. For many, their technical drawing abilities significantly improve with time. More important is that with each successful attempt the students learn that they *can* do what they previously felt they couldn't. Anyone who told them they couldn't draw have been proven wrong, including themselves. They also learn that hard work and persistence pays off, no matter the task or goal. Cuong loves telling them that the "sky is now the limit!" Nothing warms his heart more than seeing a tattooed face beaming because of that inmate's own feelings of completion and self-discovery.

In addition to his own study through Arts in Corrections, he plans to continue his unofficial drawing classes. He believes that art doesn't end for himself or anyone who takes up the challenge. He keeps profiles of all his students so that he can track their progression, showing them how far they have come. He often provides live instruction, where he and whoever is available sit together drawing a still life. Passing inmates often stop and praise their work, and no doubt taking notice that Cuong will work with anyone regardless of race. Cuong takes particular joy in breaking down prison barriers, one small chunk at a time.

Cuong is quick to point out that he has no qualifications to be an instructor. He does what he can with his limited skills and experience. He knows through Arts in Corrections the benefits of studying with a professional, working artist from the outside. He encourages his students to enroll in the official art classes, and many have followed in his footsteps. He knows first hand the rehabilitative qualities of art, and the invaluable benefit of working alongside an experienced artist who not only teaches, but more important, mentors budding artists. Cuong has seen many of his fellow inmates discover their unknown, hidden talents and creative spirit through their art practice. Their behavior and self-image are the better for the experience. Art gives them tools for self-expression, where words may have failed them in the past.

Cuong always makes time for his own art. He talks about how some of his projects take hundreds of hours to complete, making the point that "what may seem tedious to a casual observer is actually my therapy." He goes on to describe how "the noise and vulgarity of the prison environment is drowned out" by his intense concentration and focus. As he creates, his worries fade away. His family's struggles, the politics in the prison yard, the bad food; they all seem to become manageable. As he said, "If I can create a sculpture of Archangel Michael out of toilet paper, surely I can deal with some hooligans yelling outside my cell." I have heard so many artist-inmates tell me essentially the same.

Prison artists know that they are considered "outsider artists" because of their lack of formal training and professional experience. The irony for Cuong is that he is "inside." However, he doesn't think the term "outsider artist" adequately describes either him or other inmate-artists. After all, "outsider artists" have access to materials and information, unlike so many inmates who have yet to enroll in an arts program. It is true that Arts in Corrections provides materials, instructors and information, but for those who don't have access to the program, they often have to scrounge around for building materials to repurpose, and they often use hand-me-down paints. As he pointed out, "there are no instruction manuals for turning burrito wrappers into car axles." Cuong feels that his creativity and imagination have increased tenfold since he started creating in prison, and even before he gained access to Arts in Corrections. The limitations that may discourage other artists became his greatest attributes. Cuong wants to coin the term "shackled artist" as reference to anyone creating art despite his or her life conditions.

As with so many artists I've met in prison, Cuong's life journey continues, thanks in part to his creative spirit kept alive through hard work, passion, enhanced self, and the fellowship found in the art community. He doesn't know what the future holds, but he does know that art will *always* play an important part. He knows that he will always fight for the underdogs, and the misrepresented. And he will use art as his tools and weapons for change. Perhaps he is most proud to tell his parents, "I guess I became an artist after all!"

Our Racist Reality: How Ignatian Spirituality Can Help Inmates and Prison Ministers Positively Deal with the Stressors of Racism in an Inmate's Life

JOHN BOOTH[1]

"That man who is forced each day to snatch his manhood, his identity, out of the fire of human cruelty that rages to destroy it, knows … something about himself and human life that no school on earth—and indeed, no church—can teach. He achieves his own authority, and that is unshakeable."

Claudia Rankine[2]

---

[1] John T. Booth, Jr., Esq. is an attorney who has been working for the past seventeen years as an Assistant Deputy Public Defender with the New Jersey Office of the Public Defender in its Hudson County regional office. In such capacity, he has represented more than two thousand clients charged with crimes ranging in seriousness from felony possession of narcotics to capital murder. For more than a year, he has been a volunteer prison minister providing spiritual direction to the incarcerated in New York through the Jesuit organization, Thrive for Life Prison Project, Inc. He received his Bachelor of Arts from Rutgers University, New Brunswick in 1991, his Juris Doctor from Quinnipiac University School of Law in 1995 and his Master of Arts in Religious Education with a focus on spirituality and spiritual direction from Fordham University Graduate School of Religion and Religious Education in 2014.

[2] Claudia Rankine, *Citizen* (Minneapolis: Graywolf Press, 2014), 126.

On the night of Tuesday, November 8, 2016, I eventually fell asleep. I was awakened early the next morning by my Latina wife. She stroked my face awake and only stared at me. She did not say a word, yet I could sense her great fear. I asked, "Did he win?"

"Yes."

By electing someone I and many others believe is an unabashed misogynist and racist, there was no escaping the conclusion that many Americans are either sexist/racist or do not care if their president—or other people—espouse such views. As I wondered how to accept and live with this reality, I began thinking about forgotten people such as people of color and the incarcerated.

In the days following the election, I couldn't wait for Friday night when I would minister to inmates at the Manhattan Detention Complex (MDC). Several of us lay volunteers and a Jesuit brother visit the MDC, also known as "the Tombs," every Friday night. The name of our organization is the "Thrive for Life Prison Project, Inc.," which we more commonly refer to as "Thrive." With Ignatian spirituality as our guide, we lead prisoners every Friday in a meditation exercise, faith/life sharing, a closing prayer, and plenty of hugs and conversation along the way. As I awaited the Friday following the election, I thought the inmates must have felt very alone in the wake of the presidential election, especially since most are black or Latino. So many people have previously let the inmates down in many crushing ways. Now, their country let them down by electing Trump. I anticipated the inmates must have thought nobody cared for them and they don't matter. To my surprise, when I arrived that Friday, none of the inmates said anything about the election.

The following night, there was a skit on Saturday Night Live (SNL) that provided some answers to the mystery of their silence. The skit begins with a small group of young white liberal voters having an election night party and anticipating a Hillary victory. The comedian Dave Chappelle is the first black guest to arrive at this party. Toward the end of the party, Chris Rock becomes the second black guest. As everyone at the party watches the election returns on television, it slowly becomes apparent that Trump is going to win. The white guests are devastated. The black guests are not surprised at all and can't help but laugh because they know that America is racist. As black males, they have lived with the reality of racism for most, if not all their lives. The white guests are just awakening to this reality and they are distressed.[3] I wondered if this partially explained the silence of the inmates that Friday in the Tombs. Since most of the inmates are black and Latino, perhaps they felt like Chappelle and Rock who, through their use of sarcastic humor, implied it was time for white Americans to finally acknowledge that America is a racist country.[4] Perhaps long before this election, the inmates had no choice but to "grappl[e] with race and the legacy of [our county's] original sin" of slavery.[5]

As a white male, I might be able to periodically escape the issue of racism. However, my conscience and my God won't let me. If I ignore the reality of racism in our nation, I turn my back on those whom I love and for whom I care. I also turn my back on God. I would be reinforcing what racism tells its victims: "You are inferior. You do not matter." The face of my wife and those of the inmates for whom I minister compel me to do something. Their faces and God are my reality.

Up until this election, I was drawn to prison ministry because of inmates' overwhelming need for love and attention. Since the election, I feel an additional incentive for being a prison minister: to do something proactive about racism in America. In my personal journey along this particular path, I have come to a greater understanding and appreciation of the many ways in which racism negatively preys upon

---

[3] *Saturday Night Live*, season 42, episode 6, "Election Night," featuring Cecily Strong, Dave Chappelle, Aidy Bryant, Beck Bennett, Chris Rock, Vanessa Bayer, aired November 12, 2016, on NBC, accessed February 9, 2017, http://www.nbc.com.

[4] Ibid.

[5] Wesley Lowery, *They Can't Kill Us All: Fergusson, Baltimore and a New Era in America's Racial Justice Movement* (New York: Little, Brown, 2016), 13-14.

our weaknesses and makes all of us more vulnerable and in need of God's loving presence and assistance.

There are many potential ways of ministering to prisoners. I intend to share just one: the application of Ignatian spirituality behind the prison walls. This paper will first explore racism as a detrimental stressor in an inmate's life. The analysis will then focus upon how an Ignatian-based prison ministry can assist inmates in dealing with racism by renewing a sense of hope in their lives.

It cannot be stressed enough, the Ignatian approach to prison ministry is but one of many potential methods. There must be more than one approach because each inmate is unique in their needs and experience. By way of example, some inmates respond positively to religious-based programs while others are more receptive to non-religious ministries such as dance, music or art. There is no singular method that addresses all the needs of every inmate. By promoting as many approaches/programs as possible, the goal is to help inmates thrive, not just survive, in and out of prison. In its essence, that is what most ministries should be about: helping others to thrive, i.e., living a life that leans more toward positive self-fulfillment and away from negativity and acedia. Obstacles to thriving will be unique to each inmate. A minister's job is to help an inmate(s) discover such impediments. Racism is but one of many potential stressors and barriers to personal growth.

People who have suffered from racism need positive, loving attention. "Stigmatized individuals who report experiencing frequent exposure to discrimination or other forms of unfair treatment also report more psychological distress, depression, and lower levels of life satisfaction and happiness."[6] People who feel discriminated against may also come to develop a "cultural mistrust" of the discriminator's social group/category.[7] Such suffering at the hands of racism clearly

---

[6] Charles Stangor, "The Study of Stereotyping, Prejudice, and Discrimination within Social Psychology: A Quick History of Theory and Research," in *Handbook of Prejudice, Stereotyping and Discrimination*, edited by Todd D. Nelson (New York: Psychology Press, 2009), 7.

[7] Ibid.

necessitates a loving and empathic presence to remedy some of the loss of hope, self-value, and trust.

To be a more loving and empathic presence, a prison minister should understand how racism and other stressors may have contributed to an inmate's present incarceration. One resource for such understanding is the field of criminology. The criminologist, Robert K. Merton, posited in his "strain" or "anomie" theory that crime can be explained by frustration over the inability to achieve the general "culturally defined goals, purposes and interest."[8] Merton entitled this the General Strain Theory (GST). GST posits that when there is a loss/removal of "positive stimuli or introduction of negative stimuli," it "causes a strain such that, as with blocked opportunities," can lead to "criminal behavior."[9] Removal of positive stimuli can be things such as "loss of a boyfriend/girlfriend, the death of or serious illness of a friend, moving to a new school district, the divorce/separation of one's parents, suspension from school and the presence of a variety of adverse conditions at work."[10] Anecdotally, in my experience, many inmates commit crimes after losing hope due to a loss/removal of positive stimuli such as those listed above. Being aware of such potential causes of criminal behavior will help a prison minister to be more present and attentive to an inmate.

Using GST in assessing the role of race in criminality, studies have confirmed that racism is a stressor and contributing factor in criminal behavior. A 2003 criminology study using GST found "experiencing discrimination i[s] a significant predictor of [juvenile] delinquency, even after the authors 'controlled for quality of parenting, affiliation of delinquent peers, and prior conduct problems.'"[11] A prison minister

---

[8] Shaun L. Gabbidon, *Criminological Perspectives on Race and Crime* (New York: Rutledge, Taylor, Francis, 2007), 67-68.
[9] Ibid., 73.
[10] Ibid.
[11] R.L. Simons, Y.F. Chen, E.A. Stewart, and G.H. Brody, "Incidents of Discrimination and Risk for Delinquency: a Longitudinal Test of Strain Theory with an African-American Sample," *Justice Quarterly* 20, (2003):827-854, 848. Quoted in Gabbidon, *Criminological Perspectives on Race and Crime*, 75.

who is sensitive to such potential effects of racism will be effective in helping an inmate deal more positively with this issue. "Furthermore, the results showed that ... anger and depression fostered by discrimination increase(d) delinquent behavior."[12] Knowledge of this subject may also provide courage for the minister to gently explore anger/depression with an inmate. Ultimately, the more a prisoner shares with a minister and others, the more she/he may come to understand what might have contributed to their incarceration. Such insight will hopefully guide an inmate toward a more positive and fulfilling life on both sides of the wall.

Religion can help a person deal with the stressor of racism. A 2003 study analyzed whether black religiosity had any impact upon the negative effects of racism amongst black Americans. The study concluded "that individuals who are religiously committed are less likely than those who are not to engage in deviant coping in reaction to personal problems because their religiosity buffers the effects of negative emotions on deviance as well as directly and indirectly ... their coping strategies."[13] A subsequent study "also noted that social support can serve as an effective buffer against depression and anxiety."[14] Thus, the social support and religious guidance of a prison minister can help inmates address stressors/circumstances such as racism that are impeding their interior growth. (Racism is but one of many potential stressors in an inmate's life.)

Informed by such criminological studies and the fact that people of color are incarcerated at disproportionately higher rates,[15] prison ministry can assist an inmate in dealing with the negative effects of racism in their lives. A person engaged in prison ministry is uniquely

---

[12] Gabbidon, *Criminological Perspectives on Race and Crime*, 74.
[13] S.J. Jang and B.R. Johnson, "Strain, Negative Emotions, and Deviant Coping Among African-Americans: a Test of General Strain Theory," *Journal of Quantitative Criminology* 19, (2003):79-105, 98, quoted in Gabbidon, *Criminological Perspectives on Race and Crime*, 74.
[14] Gabbidon, *Criminological Perspectives on Race and Crime*, 74.
[15] Michelle Alexander, *The New Jim Crow: Mass Incarceration in the Age of Colorblindness*, rev. ed. (New York: New Press, 2012), 6-7.

situated to illuminate God's presence, love, and healing to an inmate because prisoners might perceive this outsider as someone "safe" to talk to. Although such perceptions by the inmate might not be conscious, this view may allow an outsider to draw out deeper feelings from the inmate.[16] "The caring presence of another person during a time of trial can be healing."[17] The caring presence of a prison minister will also make the minister more receptive to God's grace and "God will more easily bring his comfort [to the inmate] through [the prison minister]."[18] Just being aware of an inmate's "hidden pain" will make an outsider very effective even in a group setting.[19]

Studies have found that inmates typically practice religion for several reasons. One reason is it may provide direction, meaning, and hope in their lives. Some perceive their incarceration as the will of God and active religious practice provides an opportunity to conform their lives more closely to the will of God. Others may develop a better self-image by coming to realize they are loved by a higher being. The discipline required to practice religion may also foster greater self-control and ability to follow prison rules. Many inmates also receive a peace of mind that assists in their psychological survival behind the wall.[20]

The centrality of the *Spiritual Exercises* (the *Exercises*) in Ignatian Spirituality can inspire a ministerial presence that can soothe the wounds of racism suffered by inmates. The *Exercises* was authored by Saint Ignatius of Loyola in the sixteenth century. It is akin to a manual or "how to" book for prayerful meditations typically conducted with the assistance of a spiritual director. The fruits of the book are not

---

[16] Lennie Spitale, *Prison Ministry: Understanding Prison Culture Inside and Out* (Nashville: B&H Publishing Group, 2002), 43.
[17] Henry G. Covert, *Ministry to the Incarcerated*, 2nd ed. (La Vergne, TN: Lightning Source, Inc., 2014), 79.
[18] Spitale, *Prison Ministry*, 43.
[19] Ibid.
[20] Kumandri S. Murty, Angela M. Owens and Ashwin G. Vyas, *Voices from Prison: an Ethnographic Study of Black Male Prisoners* (Lanham, MD: University Press of America, 2004), 229-230.

realized until one applies its prayer exercises to the practice of one's spirituality.[21] Avery Dulles, S.J. succinctly surmises "[t]he overall purpose of the [*Exercises*] is to enable exercitants [those who are doing the *Exercises*] to overcome their disordered inclinations, to be enflamed with the love of God, and to make concrete resolutions about how to follow Christ more closely."[22]

Throughout the *Exercises*, Ignatius invites the exercitant to prayerfully explore her/his graced personal history in the same way one uses the Word of God: as a source of Divine revelation and guidance.[23] Praying with her/his graced history reveals how God was lovingly present in the good times, bad times and everything in between. This type of prayer personally reveals that God loves and values the exercitant dearly. It is also one way of attending to a central focus in Ignatian spirituality of "finding God in all things."[24]

The *Exercises* is meant to be experienced as a thirty-day retreat at a retreat house secluded from the "real world" or while on retreat in the "real world" over a longer period, such as thirty weeks. The thirty-day and thirty-week retreats are referred to as the Twentieth and Nineteenth Annotation[25] retreats, respectively.[26] The *Exercises* may also be experienced in a shortened version, the Eighteenth Annotation, for persons unable or unprepared for conducting the

---

[21] George E. Ganss, S.J., ed., *Ignatius of Loyola: The Spiritual Exercises and Selected Works* (Mahwah, NJ: Paulist Press, 1991), 50.

[22] Avery Dulles, S.J., preface to *The Spiritual Exercises of St. Ignatius: Based on Studies in the Language of the Autograph*, ed. John F. Thornton and Susan B. Varenne, trans. Louis J. Puhl, S.J. (New York: Random House, 2000), xvii.

[23] John J. English, S.J., *Spiritual Freedom: From an Experience of the Ignatian Exercises to the Art of Spiritual Guidance*, 2nd ed. (Chicago: Loyola Press, 1995), 271-273.

[24] Ganss, *Ignatius of Loyola*, 458-459.

[25] The word "annotation" refers to the beginning section of the *Exercises* which contain various "annotations" or preliminary observations to assist retreatants and their directors.

[26] Ganss, *Ignatius of Loyola*, 127-128.

full *Exercises*.[27] Obviously, the physical setting of a jail or prison makes giving the full form of the *Exercises* very difficult. However, Ignatian spirituality—which is rooted in the *Exercises*—along with the use of various meditations from the *Exercises*, can prove fruitful for prison ministry's attempt at healing/dealing with the wounds of racism.

Armed with Ignatian spirituality as a guide, a prison minister can help to narrow the divide of the "cultural mistrust" that racism often creates between an inmate and people more closely associated with the predominant mainstream culture. I witnessed this with one of the inmates at the Tombs. For privacy concerns, I will call him Pedro.

Pedro was one of the first inmates to join us on Friday nights in the Tombs. In the beginning he was depressed, with virtually no hope for his legal and personal circumstances. I was an outsider to Pedro and his prison/non-prison environment. By meeting with Pedro on a consistent basis, he felt comfortable confiding in me during our numerous private conversations about God and life. He eventually told me his dilemma: he didn't know if he "could trust white [jurors] to decide his case." Being a white person, I felt honored that he shared this with me. I also felt terribly about this reality. I know from my years as a public defender that the conscious and subconscious racism of prospective jurors is an ugly reality that a defendant and their attorney cannot ignore when picking a jury. There is also little an attorney can do to uncover racism in jurors. In Pedro's case, the pool from which a jury would be chosen was predominantly white and affluent. Pedro is Latino and poor.

Despite an anxious and depressive state of mind, Pedro never missed our Friday night Thrive sessions where we would lead inmates in Ignatian meditations. One meditation from the *Exercises* that Thrive uses often and has found very beneficial for prison ministry—and, for Pedro in particular—is the Examination of Conscience or

---

[27] Michael Hansen, S.J., *The First Spiritual Exercises: Four Guided Retreats* (Notre Dame, IN: Ave Maria Press, 2013), 14-15.

Consciousness, which is more commonly referred to as "the *Examen*." (The *Exercises*, as translated from their original Spanish, uses the word "conciencia," which can be translated as either "conscience" or "consciousness."[28]) Almost every Friday night at the Tombs, one of the Thrive ministers will begin this meditation by asking the inmates to close their eyes as the minister guides them in a breathing/centering exercise. Next, the minister asks them to place themselves within the presence of God. The inmates are then directed to ask for the grace to see how God is working in their lives. Then, they are prompted to share with God what they are grateful for. After this, inmates are invited to reflect upon the good and the challenging moments of the past week or few days. Lastly, they are asked to tell God what they plan to do differently in light of this examination. Once everyone has concluded their meditation, all the inmates are asked to share with the group their good and challenging moments. The ministers also encourage the inmates to engage in the *Examen* each day and to journal such prayer in notebooks provided by Thrive to the inmates.

Over time, this meditation helps inmates to more readily notice the presence of God in their lives and to respond in accordance with such knowledge. By way of example, Pedro started to overcome some of his obstacles and find a renewed sense of hope through the *Examen*. On Friday nights in the Tombs, the minister would often begin the *Examen* by asking the inmates to imagine they were on a beach and feeling the presence of God in the warmth of the sun. Occasionally, the minister would ask that they imagine meeting someone on the beach. Pedro felt too embarrassed to tell us who he met on the beach. After his transfer to another prison, Pedro sent a letter informing us that he would meet himself on that beach "and I [Pedro] would always put myself down." Eventually, Pedro would meet Jesus on the beach and they would talk. Jesus would "tell [him] that [he] was going to

---

[28] Ganss, *The Spiritual Exercises of Saint Ignatius: A Translation and Commentary* (Chicago: Loyola Press, 1992), 154, n. 30.

be okay and that when [Pedro] was ready, he would have a great life ahead of him."

After attending numerous Thrive sessions, Pedro became inspired to telephone his sister, whom he had not spoken with in years. This led to their reconciliation. At the end of his stay in the Tombs, his sister was very sad to see him transferred to a different prison, where he would be farther away and she would not be able to visit him as often.

Ultimately, Pedro won his motion to suppress. This enabled him to negotiate a much better plea deal than was previously offered because of the suppression of evidence crucial to the prosecution of his case. With a greater likelihood of a not-guilty jury verdict due to the lack of such suppressed evidence, the prosecution chose to significantly lower their plea offer for Pedro and he accepted. Pedro also avoided facing a jury.

When I last spoke with Pedro, he was awaiting transfer to another prison to serve the remainder of his sentence after having pled guilty. He thanked me for our time together. He said that because of me and my fellow ministers, he "now trusts people again." I know this only occurred by the grace of God. I like to think our presence as ministers helped Pedro become more receptive to receiving God's grace. Perhaps, Thrive's empathic presence every Friday night over many months enabled Pedro to share difficult things about faith and life with us, the inmate participants, and others. This may have fostered a renewed sense of hope in his life. As often happens in life, there may also be other unknown/unrecognized factors that contributed to Pedro's changing outlook on life. At a minimum, Thrive provided a safe and quiet place for reflection and time with God within the walls of a noisy and impersonal institution. We also provided an example of white and non-white people who care deeply about Pedro and others less fortunate than us ministers. God did the rest.

Racism is one of many pernicious obstacles that stands in the way of such inner growth of a person like Pedro. Such obstacles ultimately cause a person to think less of his or her self and can cause one to feel alienated and depressed. This was how Pedro felt when he first attended our Thrive meetings. Eventually, Pedro's time in Thrive brought him closer to God and to his sister, and reawakened his faith in other people. Most importantly, it fostered a deeper faith in himself, thanks to his hard work and the grace of God.

Although the *Examen*, and Ignatian spirituality in general, will not eliminate the negative side effects of racism and other stressors in Pedro's life, it can help him and others constructively deal with the various adversities discussed throughout this paper. At the very least, Ignatian spirituality helped Pedro find Jesus, who ministered to Pedro's negative self-perception with the hope and love of God.

Prison ministry in an Ignatian mode may not be the cure for all inmates, but it can be a lifeline for many. I firmly believe it was for Pedro. In the process of ministering to inmates, I feel I am chipping away at some of the harmful effects of racism in our country. I also believe Pedro gifted me a renewed sense of hope by helping me find one way of awakening to and coming to terms with our racist reality. There is much more work to be done if we are all going to thrive on both sides of the wall.

Hands with Bird, Ronnie Goodman, 15x15 inches, linocut, San Quentin State Prison, 2014

Truth Is...

ALISHA COLEMAN[1]

The picture I'm about to paint can only be heard,
so listen closely to every word.

Innocent until proven guilty?
They can't be serious,
In a system where
Drug dealers get more time
than serial killers,
juveniles get tried as adults,
before they become one.
I guess nobody musta warned'em
about playing with knives and guns.

Guilty by association?
That's what it's called
then they get hauled
off to the pen,
where some girls become boyz and some boyz

---

[1] Alisha Coleman is a proud member of a group of women who fight daily to make sure that women in prison receive the proper care while they're there. I'm a mother of one (daughter) who, before working for this organization, was one of the women they fought for. CCWP (California Coalition for Women Prisoners) will always be a part of me.

become women.
Sitting around
unaware of who they are,
wounded while in the belly of the beast.
I call'em invisible scars,
the kind that can't be healed
by Neosporin and stitches.

Went in walkin'
came out switching.

Could you imagine what it's like?
Being told that the beginning
is really the end of your life.
3 strikes and you're out!
Some think it's a game,
but it's really outta my hands.
Lord knows, I'm not tryna do life
on installment plans.

Everybody wanna be a part
Of the occupy system,
I need to occupy my life and
find something to do with it,
otherwise it's useless.

Some may mistake my words as verbally abusive,
But the truth is…

How do we expect our kids to grow
from concrete,
accept defeat,
have to fend for themselves
in cells where it is dark
and hot as hell?

More parents come to see kids in jail
than they do at graduations.
That's cuz the new diploma
is parole or probation

Fucked up situation
No contender.

"Now I'll be gone until November"
Listening to a public pretender
telling me to plea
Y?
Cuz I'm young, black, and sell crack in da streets.
Babies committing robbery,
1st degree.

Even with blind eyes
I could see it ain't cool.
They building prison programs
and tearing down schools.
We all got an opinion
just like we all have a choice.
No one can hear you speak
if you don't use your voice!

Afterward

Mary Wardell Ghirarduzzi

The Roundtable on Race and Incarceration, organized by the Joan and Ralph Lane Center for Catholic Studies and Social Thought and held on April 21, 2017 at the University of San Francisco, came together as an expression of our university's Jesuit mission, not as a separate diversity-related initiative or discussion. As such, this event highlights the inseparability of mission engagement and work around diversity, equity, and inclusion.

As a Chief Diversity Officer at a Jesuit University, I would like to offer four essential items for leaders at Jesuit Colleges and Universities to consider as we work to stand in solidarity with women and men who have experienced incarceration:

1) **Diversity, equity, and inclusion in Jesuit higher education must be seen and understood as an expression of our Jesuit mission.** Seeing and defending the full humanity in others is the most important mission-driven work we can do on our university and college campuses. One way for Jesuit universities to live this mission is by lifting up the narratives and stories of those who have been physically separated from society through a structural form of racism and who know from personal experience the hardship and pain perpetuated by the U.S. penal and prison system.

2) **As such, the Jesuit educational mission for the common good calls us to dismantle racism within our reach by applying an anti-racist frame in our campus policies, perspectives and practices and develop anti-racist initiatives in diversity, equity and inclusion efforts at Jesuit institutions.** It is not enough to talk about or promote diversity awareness or celebration among our students and employees. Nor is it fair to repeatedly ask people of color within our campus communities to be our educators by helping us understand through their personal narratives and witness their lived experiences and realized constructs of power, oppression, and privilege. We must all carry our cross to confront racism on campus each day. This is particularly necessary for white identified colleagues and friends on campus who must discern and seek to uncover how structures of inequity manifest in their daily lives and the lives of those around them. We must be interested and proactive by engaging in analysis in how racism functions and persists in our society and institutions. Additionally, Jesuit institutions must facilitate on-going learning experiences, especially to the lay women and men who enliven and sustain the Jesuit mission—they need tools of change to understand and ultimately dismantle systemic racism.

3) **There is a need for mission-driven anchor institutions to lead the way by telling the truth about their own historic role and participation in the legacy of exclusion and by committing to concrete actions for reconciliation.** Truth telling is a requirement for reconciliation. Each university campus has a narrative about how the campus evolved over the decades and the critical role our institutions played in the communities wherein we are situated. Would other voices tell a different narrative about the Jesuit university in their city? Our institutional storytelling, memory and recollection may need to be reexamined when applying an anti-racist frame. With our mission and identity, Jesuit institutions can stand in contrast with the limited memory of our modern culture. We need to be the embodied counter

to false or exclusionary narratives generated in the dominant K-12 curriculum of our country's educational systems that are reinforced through public policy and cultural manifestation. We must seek to understand when and how we have fulfilled our mission and when we have not fulfilled our mission and who was impacted by those institutional actions.

4) **Jesuit universities as a collective are positioned to offer society a critical understanding of mass incarceration in the United States as a modern-day form of systemic, racialized bondage.** Creating a social and cultural transformation requires critical consciousness-raising. Nobody truly comprehends the trials and tribulations of our incarcerated or formerly incarcerated brothers and sisters. We know the staggering statistics with the U.S. having the largest penal system in the world. We know the preponderance of race as a key component to the penal system and we know the obscene number of women and men of color (and their children and families) whose lives are changed forever. These individuals are the most venerable, poor, and marginalized in our American society. Jesuit universities are poised and distinctly situated to advance social transformation through scholarly pursuits and action grounded in truth and reconciliation. We can help ignite and contribute to transformative community dialogues that involve our students, faculty, and staff in community and in solidarity with others.

The essays in this volume, written by scholars, educators, activists, parents, college students, entrepreneurs, interfaith and community leaders; challenge us to reflect on systemic racism and understand more deeply how it functions in society. This critical understanding calls us to action. The mission of our Jesuit institutions, active in the minds and hearts of our students and alumni, calls us to empower the hundreds of thousands of currently and formerly incarcerated women and men who have stories to tell and are willing to share their truth with us.

DATE DUE

JAN 1 5 2020

PRINTED IN U.S.A.

CPSIA information can be obtained
at www.ICGtesting.com
Printed in the USA
BVOW09s1512130418
513215BV00001B/119/P